AUTHORITY TO HEAL

Authority to Heal

Ken Blue

MONARCH
Eastbourne

First published in the USA by
InterVarsity Press, Downers Grove, Illinois

First British edition 1989

Biblical quotations are from the
New International Version © International Bible Society
1973, 1978, 1984

Front cover design by Vic Mitchell

British Library Cataloguing in Publication Data

Blue, Ken
   Authority to heal.
    1. Christianity. Spiritual healing
   I. Title
   615.8'52

ISBN 1–85424–038–2 (Monarch)
     0–7324–0405–3 (Albatross)

Co-published in Australia by
Albatross Books, PO Box 320, Sutherland, NSW 2232

Printed in Great Britain for
MONARCH PUBLICATIONS LTD
1 St Anne's Road, Eastbourne, E Sussex BN21 3UN by
Richard Clay Ltd, Bungay, Suffolk
Reproduced from the original text by arrangement with
InterVarsity Press

To my mother, Ruth Blue,
who eagerly receives God's healing
and freely passes it on.

Acknowledgments

Many have encouraged me in this publication. I can thank only a few. My thanks first to John Wimber, who, more than any other, gave me teaching and experience in healing the sick. I hope he will recognize his influence in these pages. My gratitude also goes to Professor Ray Anderson, who asked me tough questions and then helped me find pastorally and theologically responsible answers to them. I hope that he too will recognize his influence in these pages. My friend and mentor, John White, I thank for encouraging me to publish this work and for helping me get it into acceptable form. My appreciation also to C. Peter Wagner, Peter Davids, Blaine Cook, David Cowper-Smith, Andy Le Peau and Jim Hoover, who each in his own way helped me in this effort. Finally my heartfelt gratitude to my wife, Patti, and secretary Rauna Amouzou, for typing this manuscript.

Foreword

A famous Chinese writer tells us there are two classes of author. One kind will accumulate data, sort them and draw conclusions. The other kind, faced with the same data, incorporates them into his or her life, and later is compelled to write by the urgency of a vital experience.

Consequently, there will be two classes of books. The first book has passed only through the writer's intellect; the second is the costly fruit of the writer's pains, struggles and joys. It reflects a wisdom tested in life's laboratory. To use John the apostle's expression, it is the word of the writer's testimony.

Ken Blue belongs to the second class of writer. His writing grows out of living experience rather than academic detachment. Biblical truths have to be lived before they can truly be understood. That is not to say that what he presents is merely his own experience—far from it. It accurately reflects a biblical emphasis. But in the pain and joy of living out that emphasis, his confidence in it increased, his appreciation of it deepened, and his sense of urgency as to its importance forced him to unburden himself and put pen to paper.

He shares with us, then, the fruit of his having put Scripture to the test. In view of the kind of writer Ken is, it should not surprise us that for him the basic reason we must heal the sick is that Christ commands us to. What he has to say is of more than academic interest. It reflects an urgent imperative.

Yet he does not neglect academic considerations. He deals firmly with wrong and unbiblical thinking both on the part of the advocates and the opponents of healing. For the issue in the twentieth century has divided Christians into two camps, each fighting the other with half-truths and pseudobiblical shibboleths, each arrogantly persuaded of its virtue and of its corner on truth and divine approval.

But there are now signs that healing may once again take its place in the normal life of local churches. I join Ken in praying that this book may play a part in bringing that transformation about.

John White

REDISCOVERING THE MINISTRY OF HEALING

CHRISTIANS TODAY ARE REDISCOVERING CHRIST'S MINISTRY of healing the sick, and I am one who is making that rediscovery. Along with most evangelical Christians, I have always believed the New Testament accounts of the healings performed by Jesus and his followers. Moreover, I have never found any evidence in Scripture that indicates that this ministry should or did cease with the apostles. Instead I have understood that it should continue in the church until Christ returns.

But often in the past when I prayed for the sick in my role as pastor, father or friend, most of those I prayed for did not get better and some even died. In fact, my best friend died, virtually in my arms, as I prayed as fervently as I could with all the faith I possessed.

The Bible said yes to the church's healing ministry; my experience said no. I doubted myself. Had I read the Bible correctly? Was it true that miracles of healing ceased with the apostles? Was there something wrong with my faith? Was I not righteous enough to get my prayers answered?

I doubted God. Had he promised more in the New Testament than he could or would deliver today? Did he only care about our souls but not our bodies? Did he want us to accept sickness and pain passively as a testing or refining blessing from him?

Out of sheer necessity I began to press through my doubts to find answers. The demands of my ministry forced me in the end either to learn how to heal the sick or else to find another line of work.

In the spring of 1979 I founded an evangelistic mission to the west side of the city of Vancouver, British Columbia. Little did I suspect at the time that doing effective evangelism and church planting in this community required that I be effective in healing the sick and demonized.

This urban community on the west coast of Canada is famous for its beaches, its various counterculture lifestyles, and its dense population committed to pop psychology and religious cults. The Billy Graham Evangelistic Association once targeted it as one of the least evangelized areas in North America. It was apparent to them that the residents of this community warmly embraced every type of religious orientation except the gospel of Jesus Christ.

Our mission to this area was supported and governed by a group of churches, representing most of the major denominations in Western Canada. My associates in this evangelistic outreach were skilled, creative and highly motivated. During the four years of the mission's activity, we employed every conceivable evangelistic strategy and tactic. We knocked on doors; we preached on street corners; we conducted evangelistic Bible studies in our own Christian bookstore; we promoted music concerts on the beach and in auditoriums; we did high-quality street theater; we provided social assistance to those in need; we mailed and handed out gospel literature and Bibles; we set up a neighborhood counseling service; we sent out trained workers, fifty at a time, to witness on the streets; we fasted and we prayed; and we cried out to God. These evangelistic activities were supported and strengthened by the Community Church of which I was pastor at that time.

This work was gratifying for all involved. Through our efforts some in our neighborhood became followers of Jesus, and our church grew as a result. These were significant rewards. However, our five years of work brought about little positive change in the community as a whole. The social and religious life of the local area was apparently still untouched by the gospel.

A unique difficulty we faced on our mission field was that we were just one of literally dozens of religious groups there. All of these groups preached the virtues of their various gurus and saviors. From the general community's point of view, little separated them from us. While we could point to our Holy Scripture, our prophets, our conversion experience, our community of love, acceptance and social responsibility, so could they. When we sat down with leaders from these other groups to discuss truth questions and the rational support for our beliefs, we won the day convincingly. But this seemed not to matter. We did everything humanly possible to define our distance from the other groups in order to present the unique saving gospel of Jesus Christ. But we lacked, as the Lausanne Committee for Evangelism pointed out, "signs to validate our evangelism."[1]

When the early church preached the gospel of Jesus Christ, their preaching was validated and illustrated by signs, usually in the form of healings. This combination of preaching and manifest power produced marked effects. Virtually every mass turning to God recorded in the New Testament resulted when both were present. Dispensational speculations about gifts of healings vanishing with the apostles notwithstanding, this aspect of church life and witness is not just a first-century phenomenon. J. Sidlow Baxter and Morton Kelsey amply document the continuing presence of the miraculous signs of the kingdom of God throughout church history.[2] And where the church is growing rapidly around the world today—as in mainland China, South America and Africa—there is usually both gospel preaching and power from on high to validate and illustrate that gospel.

The connection between an active healing ministry and effective evangelism holds even in the industrialized West. In his book *Power Evangelism*, John Wimber discusses this connection in North America. Canon Jim Glennon of Sydney, Australia, has for the past twenty-five years directed a healing ministry which is now the largest Anglican ministry of its type in the world. He recently told me that in his church more people have been won to Christ through healing than by all other means combined.

As we reflected on our own circumstances, in contrast with the rapidly expanding church of the New Testament and in other parts of the world today, it was clear that we needed to operate the way they do.

Our need to participate in more of the signs of the kingdom of God, particularly healing and deliverance, intensified as we tried to integrate new believers into our church. Many young people from our community wanted to follow Jesus but were in bondage to drugs and alcohol. Some were deeply involved in the occult. A few, both men and women, were prostitutes. No amount of counseling and community support could significantly help many of them. They needed to be spiritually, physically and emotionally healed and delivered from powerful bondages. It was then I became determined to find someone to train me in praying for the sick and demonized.

Shortly after my search began I heard about the "Signs, Wonders and Church Growth" course offered by Fuller Seminary, and I signed up. This class, taught by John Wimber and Peter Wagner, proved to be my launching pad into the ministry of healing. It provided me with enough information and practical experience to get started. The first several months of praying for the sick were frustrating, but, as time passed, I saw more and more people healed, some dramatically. I was on my way.

Initially, I wanted to learn about healing and deliverance to authenticate the gospel in evangelism and carry on effective pastoral care. These original motives were soon joined by others. I found that common human compassion became a compelling reason to pray for the sick. It was also exhilarating to be God's agent in relieving illness and pain. Praying for the sick and seeing them helped was and is intensely gratifying.

Gradually, however, I came to what for me is the essential motive to pray for the sick. I had read the Bible for fifteen years but had never noticed that when Jesus told his followers to preach the kingdom of God, he also commanded them to heal the sick and to cast out demons (Lk 9:1-2; 10:8-9; Mt 10:7-8; Mk 6:12-13). I preached the gospel because I saw that the Lord commanded this. Now I realized that in the same breath, he also commanded me to heal the sick and cast out demons. Whether or not healing aids in evangelism, or whether or not this ministry is enjoyable or even works, I do not intend to ever stop. I understand now that the command to pray for the sick is one which I cannot explain away or ignore.

What began as a need for more effective evangelism produced a changed lifestyle. My prayer life in general has been renewed. My Bible reading has become a real adventure now, too. Many passages of the New Testament that I previously handled more or less metaphorically have become immediate and concrete to me. I now see and touch what before seemed distant and unreal. Moreover, I myself have received substantial physical and inner healing as a result of my involvement in a healing ministry.

As I began to instruct and train others in healing the sick, I developed my own teaching material. I wanted to develop a theology and model of ministry consistent with my evangelical doctrinal beliefs and convictions. The theology and model of ministry presented in this book have been taught in over one hundred conferences and church meetings. As a result of this field testing, the material has been rewritten many times and the model of healing refined.

I trust that what follows here will continue to be tested, tried and improved by those more competent and experienced than I.

The first of the four parts of this work is a critical analysis of several approaches to healing. I label these approaches "theological hindrances" because they are pastorally irresponsible, they are inconsistent with Scripture and, in general, they undermine the healing ministry of the church.

Part two is a theological analysis of God's intent to, and means of, healing the sick. I first examine how our view of God's will in sickness and healing determines our effectiveness in ministry. I then assert that God's will regarding sickness and healing is disclosed to us in the Incarnation of his Son.

I then examine the relationship of the coming of the kingdom of God in Jesus to the healing ministry of the modern church. Evil's power to make sick and the church's authority to make well are discussed here, as well as the issue of God's sovereignty and Christian faith in the process of healing.

In the third part I discuss models of Christian healing. I offer here a practical, five-step model of healing which may be implemented into the life of most Christian congregations. This model provides the individual minister and healing team with a structure for ministry. It gives the minister a place to start, a way to continue and a place to stop in praying for the sick. I follow this with a discussion of the complexity and wholeness of human beings in relationship to healing and conclude with a call to obedience in carrying Jesus' healing ministry forward.

What I write here is offered to help individual Christians and local congregations to get started and be further equipped in the ministry of healing the sick. As God continues to restore more of the signs of the kingdom to our church communities, I invoke again an ancient prayer whose author remains unknown:

> From cowardice that shrinks from new truth, from laziness that is content with half-truth, from arrogance that thinks it knows all truth, O God of Truth, deliver us.

PART 1

CLEARING THE GROUND
OF THEOLOGICAL HINDRANCES

IN OUR WORLD WEEDS AND THORNS THRIVE WITH-
out any help from us. Fruit trees and vegetable plants, however, need
our constant attention merely to survive. This spring I planted a
garden in our back yard. Before I could sow seed in the ground, my
sons and I had to clear it of weeds and thorns which had grown up
over the winter. I then planted good seed which sprouted and ma-
tured and is now ready to harvest. In preparing ourselves to pray for
the sick, the same sort of weeding process must occur in our thinking. Before good theological and biblical seed can be planted in our
hearts, certain weeds and thorns must first be rooted out.

The New Testament leaves no doubt about the church's authority
over Satan, sin and sickness. Yet the people of God today lack much
of that original assurance and power, partly because certain errone-

ous ideas have taken root in our thinking. These weeds and thorns make us ineffective by confusing and inhibiting us. In the parable of the sower (Mt 13; Mk 4; Lk 8), the good seed of the kingdom of God is sometimes choked out by weeds and thorns and prevented from maturing. In the church today, the necessary discernment and confidence needed for effectively praying for the sick are likewise restricted.

In this section I will identify theological hindrances undermining the healing ministry in the church today. As I discuss theological hindrances to healing, I will be introducing a positive, empowering theology of healing to replace them.

CHAPTER ONE

SANCTIFICATION THROUGH SICKNESS

W HAT WE WOULD CALL CHILD ABUSE IN A HUMAN FAMILY, some have labeled a blessing in the family of God. Francis MacNutt explains:

> When we say that God sends sickness or asks us to endure it, we are creating for many people an image of God they must eventually reject. What human mother or father would choose cancer for their daughter in order to tame her pride? . . . Those preachers and chaplains who try to comfort the sick by telling them to accept their illness as a blessing sent from God are giving an immediate consolation, but at what an ultimate cost! . . . In a sense, we unwittingly treat God as something like a pagan deity, placated by human sacrifice.[1]

One of the greatest hindrances to a vital healing ministry in the church today is the notion that sickness is essentially good for us, that it is sent to us to purify the soul and build character. For this reason, many believers consider it better to endure illness than to be healed. Accepting the "cross of sickness" is seen as Christlike; seeking healing is seen as selfish. And so, many who could be healed are not, simply because they think they shouldn't be.

The Roots of Sanctification through Sickness

The roots of this kind of thinking can be traced back to the Roman persecution of the church during the second and third centuries. These first bloody persecutions precipitated a crisis of faith within the early church. Theologians and lay people alike struggled to make sense of what they regarded as a contradiction. Christ, they believed, should be victor over his enemies, yet now his enemies appeared to be winning the battles.

They resolved the tension of this apparent contradiction by finding dignity and purpose in their suffering. Second- and third-century Christians began to see that, though Jesus really had ascended to his kingly throne, false rulers of this world continued to resist his authority by persecuting his true followers. Their suffering showed that they were faithful to their king.

So the early church learned to value suffering. They also began to observe its practical benefits. The Roman persecution seemed to purify and multiply the church's membership. Any among them who were insincere or halfhearted fell away, and yet the church grew in number. Thus Tertullian declared, "The blood of the martyrs is the seed of the church." I observed these same positive effects of persecution to the body of Christ while serving as a missionary in Communist East Europe.

Persecution became so highly valued in the early church that, according to New Testament scholar Peter Davids, a virtual cult of martyrdom developed between A.D. 100 and 300.[2] Suffering, and especially dying, for the faith brought the sufferer higher status. The church had three classes during this period: (1) the outcasts who compromised to avoid suffering, (2) the majority who did not suffer much persecution or who fled persecution, and (3) the "confessors" who were imprisoned or martyred for their faith.

Roman persecution of the church (which was always sporadic) officially stopped during the time of Constantine. As Christians made alliances with the state and eventually became the privileged class, some believers became concerned. First, they noted that as Christianity became the official religion of Rome, its moral and spiritual standards dropped. Second, apart from persecution they lacked the means to attain the status of a martyr.

In response to this dual concern, many fled to the desert to practice asceticism. Without state-sponsored persecution, the true "confessors" would have to persecute themselves. The self-persecution of the ascetics was inflicted through prolonged fastings, exposure to the elements, sleep deprivation and the neglect of basic hygiene. Naturally enough, sickness often resulted. So in the minds of some, sickness became synonymous with the suffering of the true "confessors" and therefore was viewed positively.

The belief that it is spiritually profitable to degrade the body was spuriously validated and promoted by Greek philosophy. Greek thinking maintains a dichotomy between spirit and matter—the former seen as good; the latter, as evil. Under Greek influence in the third and fourth centuries A.D., the church began to view the body more and more with contempt. It was taught that anything which curbed the body's pleasures and comfort, such as sickness, was good for the soul. Thus Greek thinking provided fertilizer for the ascetic notion of "sanctification through sickness."

In summary, the early church first came to terms with and then embraced suffering under persecution. When state-sponsored persecution ceased, suffering continued in the form of self-persecution which often resulted in sickness, which in turn became associated with the sanctifying effects of the initial persecution. With Greek

philosophy validating these erroneous attitudes, the notion of "sanctification through sickness" became firmly rooted in the church.
With sickness viewed as a possible benefit to spiritual formation,
praying for healing became less frequent.

The church's shift away from the ministry of physical healing was
reflected in the way the church began to interpret Scripture. The
healing passages in the New Testament were interpreted in terms of
the soul. For instance, James 5:13-18, which clearly refers to physical
healing, was used to support the notion of "last rights" or "extreme
unction." Here the prayer offered in faith to "make the sick person
well" (Jas 5:15) was reinterpreted to say "make the sick soul well
from sin" in preparation for the death of the body. Contrary to the
clear meaning of the text, there was no expectation or even desire
that the sick person should be physically healed.

Firmly rooted in church doctrine, "sanctification through sickness" survived the Reformation intact. The Reformation put aside
"extreme unction" because of its sacramental trappings, but a basic
ambivalence toward the body remained. Sickness was still valued for
its spiritual benefits. Life was viewed as a preparation for the after-
life. Sickness was regarded as a help in this preparation.

In the sixteenth century, for instance, the Church of England
included these words in the office for the visitation of the sick:
"Wherefore, whatsoever your sickness is, know you certainly that it
is God's visitation." And the reason for this visitation is that "your
faith may be found in the day of the Lord laudable, glorious and
honorable . . . or else it be sent unto you to correct and amend in
you whatsoever doth offend the eyes of your heavenly Father."[3]

The wedding of the European Protestant church to sickness
seemed so strong to Friedrich Nietzsche that he spitefully asserted:
"Christianity needs sickness." And "making sick is the true hidden
objective of the church's whole system of salvation procedures."[4]
Inevitably, where illness is valued for the spiritual good it is sup-
posed to bring, prayer to heal the sick will be weak or nonexistent.

Sanctification through Sickness Today

Many in the church today still believe that sickness should be embraced and healing should not be sought. I recently debated an eminent theologian on the issue of praying for the sick. At one point he was asked if he didn't think "a healing emphasis was a good thing, especially in some churches where it is virtually nonexistent?" He responded:

> I'm not at all sure. I think it was much healthier in the old days when people didn't expect healing but emphasized the spiritual value, the maturing effect of the discipline of suffering. . . . I think that you end up poorer, not richer, less mature rather than more spiritual when you expect healing.[5]

Such an attitude obviously inhibits healing prayer.

I recently met a seminary student I will call Richard, who had suffered a stroke that left the right side of his body virtually paralyzed. When I offered to pray for him, he thanked me for my concern but declined. He then explained how, in his affliction, he had grown close to God and therefore regarded partial paralysis as a good thing. I agreed with him on what seemed to be a significant positive benefit and then suggested that if the stroke had been of value, how much more the healing of it would be of value! He thought over what I said but still declined my praying for him because, as he said, "I don't want to miss out on anything God wants to teach me through this." I suggested that some of what God wished to teach him might come through healing.

I then asked Richard if he took physical therapy to improve his condition. He said yes, of course he did. I then asked why he would accept improvement for his condition through therapy but not through prayer. After a long pause, he shrugged his one good shoulder and said, "I don't know."

When we get sick or hurt, we go to the doctor and expect him to help us. We never question whether or not it is God's will for us to go. We presume that it is proper to get medical help and for that help to be effective. Why then are we reluctant to seek help through spiritual means?

When pressed to justify the "sanctification through sickness" theory, its exponents often sight the educational or remedial value of sickness. The Bible offers some support for this. God does occasionally send physical affliction to correct the behavior of his people. But when God afflicts his people, he tells them what behavior he wants to correct. People are not long in doubt about what to do to be healed.

Paul, for instance, was struck blind (Acts 9:1-9). This divinely inflicted ailment proved essential to his conversion from persecuting Christ to serving Christ; it was therefore educational and remedial. Following the appropriate change in Paul's attitude and behavior, he was healed (Acts 9:17-18).

When God sends sanctifying sickness, it is sent to modify bad behavior. When the behavior is remedied, the sickness is healed. In the case of the sickness and death visited upon the Corinthian church (1 Cor 11:27-31), Paul made it abundantly clear that this was punishment for sin and thus it was educational. But the Corinthians were not to passively accept this sickness, but rather they were to stop sinning against the Lord's Supper and be healed. They were not to view this sickness as anything other than a strong encouragement to stop sinning.

This approach makes perfect sense. A parent's discipline is only fair and helpful if the child knows what it is for. If a parent repeatedly strikes a child without explanation, there is no educational value in it. Such "discipline" might even teach the child that the parent is unpredictably cruel. Sickness is rarely seen in Scripture as a divine means of educating God's people. But when sickness is used to educate, it lasts only as long as the sin continues and not interminably without explanation, as chronic illness often does.

Other defenders of "sanctification through sickness" suggest that sickness is often given to us as a cross which God expects us to bear bravely. This notion carries a pious ring, but when we examine it in light of the biblical teaching on cross-bearing we spot its error. The New Testament clearly teaches that cross-bearing is voluntary. It was for Jesus, and it is for us (Mt 16:24; Lk 9:23). And not only is cross-bearing voluntary, it is active and not passive. On the other hand, getting sick or disabled is rarely voluntary, nor is it actively sought by mentally healthy people.

Akin to cross-bearing as a justification for illness is the idea that sickness is a "test" sent by God. A person in the midst of such a test may be temporarily consoled with the words "God must trust you to send you such a test." But on reflection such a person might wish to have been less trusted by God and therefore less tested. And like the idea that sickness is educational, so the idea that sickness is a test is valid only if one learns the reason for the test and whether the test has been passed or failed. Rarely is such information provided to the chronically ill person.[6]

It is manifestly true that some people are sanctified through sickness, as people may be through any and all of life's painful experiences, "because we know that in all things God works for the good of those who love him" (Rom 8:28). Nothing I have said thus far has in any way been meant to deny this. However, we are not to receive sickness passively as if it were good in and of itself. We are instead to fight it with all we have, and the church has Christ's ministry of healing with which to fight it.

Suffering and Sickness

But someone may object at this point, saying that the New Testament teaches that suffering is inevitable, that it may be good for us, and that on occasion we are to accept it. I would respond with a qualified yes. In the New Testament, *suffering* is sometimes presented positively but *sickness* never is. This distinction is vitally important. Let me explain. Modern English usage collapses sickness into the concept of suffering, but the New Testament clearly distinguishes sickness from suffering. In the New Testament, *sickness* is sickness and *suffering* always refers to the pain of persecution inflicted by persons or demons.

The *pascho* word group in the New Testament is translated "suffering" in our English Bibles. Of the sixty-five appearances of words from this group in the New Testament, only one has to do with physical sickness, and in that case (Mt 17:15) the illness (epilepsy?) is ascribed to a demon! In Mark 5:26, the term *suffer* applies not to the woman's illness but to her treatment by the physicians! The New Testament consistently defines suffering as some sort of persecution and not as physical sickness. We are told that persecution has value and merit. We are never told this about sickness.

The New Testament is also clear about the distinctly different ways we are to respond to suffering under persecution as opposed to sickness. Suffering persecution is inevitable for the true disciple, and there are a variety of ways to respond to it. We may resist it on one occasion, flee from it on another, and accept it on yet another. Sickness on the other hand is not in this same way an effect of true discipleship. It is not inevitable, and we are always to fight it.

In the book of Acts for instance, suffering due to persecution is the result of boldness in proclaiming Christ (Acts 4:1-22; 5:40-42; 7:54—8:3; 14:19-20; and so forth). Consequently, suffering may have to be endured bravely or even joyfully. "The apostles left the Sanhedrin, rejoicing because they had been counted worthy of suffering disgrace [flogging] for the Name" (Acts 5:41). On the other hand, the early church sometimes prayed to be delivered from persecution (Acts 12:5). Occasionally they were delivered; other times not.

But the ambiguity surrounding persecution is not present with regard to sickness. Never do we find New Testament Christians reconciled to sickness, enduring it patiently or rejoicing in it as they sometimes did with persecution. And while some of the prayers in Acts for deliverance from persecution were not answered positively, the prayers for healing always were.

One of the clearest biblical distinctions between suffering and sickness is found in the book of James. James says, "Consider it pure joy . . . whenever you face trials of many kinds" (Jas 1:2), but in 5:14-15 we hear James ask, "Is any one of you sick? He should call the elders of the church to pray. . . . And the prayer offered in faith will make the sick person well." The New Testament teaches us sometimes to endure suffering but always to pray to heal sickness.

English-speaking Christians need to remember that our term *suffer* has a semantic field which includes sickness. In the New Testament, however, suffering and sickness are distinct and different from each other. So the values of suffering in the New Testament should not be ascribed to sickness.[7]

Throughout this book, I seek to steer clear of abstractions and speculations about sickness and God's will regarding it. My method in getting at these questions whenever possible is to discuss what Jesus said and did about them, because in Jesus Christ the will of God is truly spoken and done.

Jesus' teaching on the proper response to suffering under persecution is ambiguous. On one occasion he said flee if persecuted (Mt 10:23). On another occasion he said actively submit to it (Mt 5:39). But no such ambiguity can be found in Jesus' teaching regarding sickness. Sickness is never viewed by him as anything but bad, and he never dealt with sickness in any way but to heal it. Nowhere in Scripture does Jesus sanction sickness for anyone for any reason. He never counseled anyone to accept sickness as inevitable or profitable. More to the point, Jesus never inflicted sickness on anyone to accomplish some higher good, although he often healed existing illness for that very reason (Jn 9). Jesus made it clear that sickness is an enemy not a friend. When possible, it is to be healed and not accepted. The New Testament scholar Ulrich Mueller asserts:

Sickness contradicts the salvation will of the creator God, who wants life and not death. That is why Jesus wanted to save the

concrete person in his life, i.e., strengthen and maintain him. . . .
This religious aspect does not give Jesus occasion to preach surrender to sickness, but rather provokes his resistance to it. . . .
Nowhere do we find the admonition to tolerate sickness, and to
come to terms with it.[8]

Jesus' response to sickness was to heal it. He said, "The thief comes
only to steal and kill and destroy; I have come that they may have
life, and have it to the full" (Jn 10:10). Sickness is not a blessing—
the One who came to defeat it is a blessing.

A Thorn in the Flesh

If there is an exception to the New Testament's explicit hostility
towards sickness, it is to be found in 2 Corinthians 12:7, where Paul
tells about his "thorn in the flesh." The thorn was given to Paul to
keep him from becoming conceited. Some Christians suggest that
this thorn is a physical sickness or affliction which was given in
order to accomplish some higher spiritual good. If the "sanctification through sickness" theory has any biblical sanction, it is here.
The problems in finding justification for it even here, however, are
formidable.

One of the many reasons for doubting that Paul's thorn was a
physical affliction is the background of the phrase in the Old Testament. In Numbers 33:55, "thorns in the sides" of God's people
refers to the harassment and persecution which Israel's neighbors
inflict on them. These nations are referred to again as thorns in
Joshua 23:13 and in Ezekiel 28:24. The Old Testament concept of
a "thorn in the flesh" refers to persecution and harassment, not
sickness.

Now notice the context of Paul's thorn in 2 Corinthians 12. In
the previous two chapters, Paul speaks of his being persecuted and
harassed by false prophets and political and religious authorities.
This discussion of his suffering at their hands leads directly into his
discussion of his "thorn in the flesh." In Paul's Hebrew mind, a

"thorn in the flesh" carried an idiomatic meaning much like "pain in the neck" does to us. It connoted personal persecution, and this is the very context of his mention of it in 2 Corinthians 12. While it is impossible to state with certainty what Paul's thorn was precisely, it is much more likely the painful opposition of personal enemies than physical affliction.[9]

But even if someone yet holds to the theory that Paul's thorn refers to physical sickness, we would still have great difficulty in saying that this supports the idea of "sanctification through sickness." We are often rightly warned not to base any doctrine on one passage of Scripture even if that passage is clear and unambiguous. How then could we be justified in sanctioning the value of sickness on one highly problematic and obscure passage?

Even if we should go to the extreme of basing a doctrine on one obscure passage, we must contend with the fact that Paul vigorously rejected his thorn at first. Three times he earnestly "pleaded with the Lord to take it away" (2 Cor 12:8). Whatever his thorn was, Paul fought it and repeatedly pleaded with God to remove it. Paul came to accept his thorn only after a bitter spiritual battle against it, and even then he accepted it only after the Lord told him specifically to do so. It seems to me that this comports with the testimony of someone like Joni Eareckson Tada, who initially sought healing for her paralysis. She fully believed God could heal her, and she aggressively went after it. She did not passively accept her condition. Only after a long spiritual battle did she feel that she must finally be reconciled to her weakness and find God's strength sufficient in it.

Jesus never preached surrender to sickness and neither should we. There are many among us who could be healed if only we would pray for them. I am someone who for years suffered chronic back pain, having accepted it as a divine means of taming my pride. Only after I was delivered of this erroneous notion was I effectively prayed for and completely healed. Our theology must sometimes be healed before our bodies can be.

CHAPTER TWO

DIVINE DETERMINISM

A YEAR AGO ONE OF MY CLOSE FRIENDS WAS DYING OF EM-physema. He staunchly believed that God controlled all aspects of his life, including his sickness. At first when I offered to pray for him, he declined, saying, "If God wants me well, he will heal me." Later on, after hearing me teach about healing, he came for prayer, announcing, "O.K., I now believe that God *wants* me well. So pray for me." I did, and soon he was healed not only of his emphysema, but of his long addiction to cigarettes, which had caused his illness in the first place.

My friend's story illustrates another theological hindrance that often needs clearing away before healing can take place. The same attitude toward suffering can be found in this letter to the editor of the L.A. *Times,* October 3, 1982. It was submitted by the pastor of a church in Beverly Hills, California, in response to a *Times* article on the theological problems of suffering.

> I feel compelled to affirm that any view of God which denies that He controls all events makes the idea of God irrelevant. . . . The real question is not "why does God allow suffering?" but "why does God show mercy at all?" God loves some of us and He does not love others in the same way. That is why there is suffering for some and salvation for others.

This statement is an extreme expression of a particular strain of Christian thought. It may sound irresponsible, yet many of us think the same way. When we say "God controls all events," we logically imply that he decrees pain or comfort wherever they are found. I identify this kind of thinking as "divine determinism" and believe it stands as a major theological hindrance to healing because, if held consistently, it makes prayer for the sick futile or irrelevant. *Futile,* since if God has decreed sickness, no amount of prayer may alter that state. Or, on the other hand, *irrelevant,* since if God has decreed healing, it will become a reality with or without prayer.

"Divine determinism" is probably most frequently found among those who identify themselves as Calvinists, though this kind of thinking is by no means confined to Calvinists alone, nor would all Calvinists succumb to the dangers it poses. Its influence can be seen throughout church history. Many New England Puritans, for example, opposed inoculation against dreaded smallpox on the grounds that sickness was in God's providence. They actually argued that to prevent smallpox was to thwart God's judgment.[1] Others later opposed the use of chloroform to relieve the pain of childbirth for the same reason.

Pastoral Problems

The pastoral problems related to "divine determinism" are not, however, behind us. Bev, a single mother, was told some years ago that her son had leukemia. She was confident that God could do anything for anyone, but her question was, Will he do something for my son? Confused about whether or not God intended to heal her child, she called for the elders of her church to come and pray, which they reluctantly did.

Later Bev recounted to me her elders' concerted effort to avoid any hint of presumption upon God's will by liberally lacing their prayers with "if it please thee, Lord" and "according to thy will" and "if it be thy will." She remembered these as prayers of doubt and not as prayers of faith. Shortly following the meeting, her son went into the hospital for the last time. After his death, she fought desperately to reconcile her lifelong devotion to a God who could have healed her son but chose not to.

In the midst of her schizophrenic struggle to love a God who had killed her son, an older woman from the church said to her, "While we don't understand why, this too fits into God's secret plan." This statement served to crystallize the issue in the young mother's mind. She knew from that moment on that she wanted nothing more to do with a God who used the painful, humiliating death of a six-year-old boy for some higher, hidden purpose.

A missionary who recently returned from the tropics told me that during the last year of his assignment, "the Lord took" his eight-year-old daughter. She had died of diphtheria. He too adhered to "divine determinism" and so painfully looked to find God's providence in the events surrounding the death of his child. When asked what he would do if he caught a man deliberately infecting his daughter with the bacillus that killed her, he said, "I would break that snake's neck with my bare hands." Further counseling revealed that in addition to the agony of losing his daughter, he suffered the guilt of not knowing how to pray for her when she was sick. Subconsciously this man had begun to hate the God he once loved and trusted.

This kind of thinking not only chokes out the viability of healing prayer during sickness, it also poisons the heart in the process. In commenting on this, Pastor Russell Dicks observes:

> If you believe, as traditional Christianity has taught, that God is sovereign . . . that is to say, He personally and with careful foresight determines the birth, the health, the handicap or freedom from handicap of every baby, that He sends the illnesses, that He determines the major events of each person's life . . . then resentment towards God in some form or another is inevitable.[2]

We will not develop such resentment, however, if we remember that God reveals himself to us in Scripture as a loving, heavenly Father. Think for a moment what happens when a Christian mother is awakened at 2:00 A.M. by the groaning of her child with a stomachache or a high fever. Does she stop to wonder if it is the Father's will to comfort her child? No, of course not. She immediately reaches for the medicine cabinet or the phone to get the doctor. In doing this, every mother declares her confidence in the rightness that her child be healed.

Why then are we confused over the question of God's will to heal when we pray for the sick? A Christian should no more hesitate to pray for healing or to ask for prayer than to call the doctor for appropriate medical care. Neither prayer nor medical attention can guarantee 100 per cent effectiveness, but we should never suppose that our Father in heaven is less concerned for the health of his children than we are for ours.

Another major difficulty with "divine determinism" is its logical inconsistency with the way we view God's will in other areas of Christian concern. For instance, we would never suggest today that by rejecting the gospel we fulfill the will of God. We believe that God is not willing that any should perish, but that all should come to repentance (2 Pet 3:9).

This conviction regarding God's will and evangelism, however, is a recent development among evangelicals. Our spiritual fathers and mothers prior to the modern missionary movement believed something quite different. They taught that if God wanted the heathen in India saved, he would save them himself without the gospel preaching of William Carey or anyone else. We marvel today that our spiritual forebears could have questioned the necessity of preaching to accomplish God's will in saving the lost. Do you suppose our children will marvel that some of us should have questioned the necessity of prayer to accomplish God's will in healing the sick?

"Divine determinism," then, undermines healing prayer by breeding despair and passivity. It proves to be pastorally destructive by fostering hostility towards God. Beyond this, it is logically inconsistent with the way we regard God's will in other areas of Christian endeavor. The most telling critique of this pattern of thought for evangelicals, however, is that it runs contrary to the reality of life as seen in the Scripture.

Human Choices

Human history, as the Bible reveals it, is determined not simply by the decrees of a sovereign God but to a large extent by the choices of people. When these choices go contrary to God's will, God's will is not done. In addressing God's people, Peter says, "You stiff-necked people. . . . You are just like your fathers: You always resist the Holy Spirit!" (Acts 7:51). In Matthew 23:37, Jesus laments the frustration of God's will by his own people: "O Jerusalem, Jerusalem, you who kill the prophets and stone those sent to you, how often I have longed to gather your children together, . . . but you were not willing." In Mark 6:5, the evangelist reports bluntly that Jesus was prevented from doing God's will (working miracles) in his hometown specifically because of his neighbors' resistance.

In 1 Timothy 2:4, Paul tells us God our Savior "wants all men to be saved and to come to a knowledge of the truth," but not all do come to a knowledge of the truth. In the same vein the apostle Peter assures us that God does not want "anyone to perish, but everyone to come to repentance" (2 Pet 3:9). According to Peter and Paul,

God wills everyone to be saved, but the reality of hell is grim testimony that his will in this is thwarted.

Similarly, Paul tells the church in Thessalonica that "it is God's will that you should be holy." Many of them obviously were not, and so God's will was at least temporarily frustrated. Since God's will is not necessarily done in other realms, why do we suppose that it is done in regard to sickness?

When the Bible speaks of God's sovereignty, it does not mean that God predetermines and controls all the events of history. God's will shall one day be done on earth as it is in heaven, but that time has not yet come. Now God is often opposed by people and a significant number of angels. As we shall see more fully in part two, we currently live between the time of Christ's victory over Satan and human sin and the final consummation of that victory.

During this intermediate period, things happen to us apart from the will of God. Some events are accidents; others result from a chain of causes which make them inevitable. Still other evils are the aftermath of choices made by humans and angels. Therefore to say that every sickness, accident, sin or stupidity happens because God wills it is at most inadequate. And expressions like God "permits" or "allows" certain bad things to happen are at best crude attempts to account for a reality we know little about.

This is not to say, however, that God is checkmated or baffled by evil. Despite accident, sin and stupidity, which causes most sickness in the world, "God works for the good of those who love him, who have been called according to his purpose" (Rom 8:28). The apostle Paul, who wrote this, experienced it first in his own life. Years before his letter to the Romans, Paul found himself preaching the gospel to the pagans in Galatia and planting a church there because of a physical illness (Gal 4:13). God sometimes uses the sickness of his servants in accomplishing some great good.

Most of you reading this will know the masterful way God works for the good in and through the physically damaged body of Joni

Eareckson Tada. She was paralyzed by accident, yet that did not stop God from working through her, nor did it stop her from obeying him. The result is immense good to her and thousands of others.

For the past two years, some friends and I have prayed for a severely retarded child. He has shown no improvement to date, but during our visits to him we come into contact with his immediate and extended family. The result is that fourteen of them have come to know and follow Jesus.

My goddaughter Jessica is deaf. It has never occurred to me that her condition is God's will or that I should stop praying that he heal her. At the same time, her parents, as a result of her illness, have been thrust into the subculture of deaf people. This in turn has opened up a fruitful ministry for them there.

Simply because God does not will illnesses nor predestine them does not mean that he no longer accomplishes his will despite them and even through them.

God works through the sickness resulting from accident, sin and stupidity to accomplish his will. He also works through his obedient people to remove these causes of suffering. Throughout the Old Testament, the Lord commands his people to eliminate specific kinds of pain. He gives them laws to seal those commands and appoints kings to enforce them. When a king fails to enforce such laws, God sends prophets to warn him. If king and people still refuse to obey God's commands to right various wrongs, the Lord sovereignly judges and punishes them. God is clearly on the side of those who suffer, and he equips his people to minister to them.

Jesus' Attitude

Scripture makes clear that God stands against human suffering in general, but how do we best determine his attitude regarding sickness and healing in particular? The clearest and fullest view of God's attitude towards sickness and healing is found in his Son Jesus Christ. As we read the record of his earthly ministry, we find God's desire in this matter unambiguously disclosed.

In Luke 13:10-15, for instance, Jesus heals a woman who "had been crippled by a spirit for eighteen years" (v. 11). It was by Satan's will that the woman was sick. It is Jesus, acting in accordance with God's will, who heals her. The synagogue ruler, thinking that he is upholding God's will in this issue, unwittingly sides with Satan saying that the woman should have remained sick on the Sabbath. It is Satan's will to cripple. It is God's will to heal. Unfortunately many religious people are confused on these points.

When we want to understand God's will, we should not try to deduce it from the circumstances of a fallen world. Neither should we form an abstract concept of God's will from a nonbiblical notion of divine sovereignty. Rather, we should look at Jesus, who is the explicit declaration of God's will.

In reflecting on the ministry of Jesus Christ, the great English preacher Leslie Weatherhead observed:

> [Jesus] seems to have regarded God's ideal purpose for every man as perfect health of body, mind and spirit, and although that ideal integration was seldom attained, Christ worked for it and believed Himself to be doing in this way the will of God.[3]

Despite the fact that God wills to heal the sick, not all the sick are healed. This ambiguity forces us to realize that we are dealing with a mystery: we are interacting with a sovereign and free God; we are confronting sin, demonic beings, and a host of complex psychological, physical and spiritual factors.

We will wrestle with these and related issues in parts two and three. As we continue, it will become clear that even though God has not disclosed all the secrets of evil, he has equipped and commanded us to overcome it. We will see that if we do not confidently and aggressively pray for the sick, we have not recognized the comprehensive nature of Christ's victory over evil nor have we seen the comprehensive nature of our assignment as followers of Jesus.

CHAPTER THREE

FAITH FORMULA

CAN-DO" AMERICAN OPTIMISM HAS FUSED WITH CHRISTIAN fundamentalism to spawn a triumphalistic theological hybrid, both attractive and dangerous. The following story was reported by Dr. Paul Brand in the November 25, 1983, issue of *Christianity Today:*

David Gilmore told about an illness of his 15-month-old son, Dustin Graham Gilmore, that began in April of 1978. At first the child came down with flu-like symptoms. The Gilmores took him to their church and the pastor prayed for him. Members of that church believed that faith alone heals any disease and that to look elsewhere for help—for example, to medical doctors—demonstrates a lack of faith in God. Gilmore and his wife followed the church's advice and simply prayed for their son. Over the next weeks they prayed faithfully as his temperature climbed, prayed when they noticed he no longer responded to sounds, and prayed harder when he went blind.

On the morning of May 15, 1978, the day after the pastor preached an especially rousing sermon about faith, the Gilmores went into their son's room and found his body a blue color, and still. He was dead. Again they prayed, for their church also believed the power of prayer can raise the dead. But Dustin Graham Gilmore stayed dead. An autopsy revealed the infant died from a form of meningitis that could have been treated easily.

This tragedy magnifies the destructive effects of the hindrance to healing I refer to here as "faith formula." It distresses me to criticize any teaching which exhorts us to stand on God's promises. I welcome the call to aggressive faith, but when faith becomes a technique to manipulate the power of God, it becomes destructive. This kind of thinking first choked out the discernment of the Gilmores, then it took the life of their son, and finally, through the media coverage of this event and others like it, it has closed off the minds of many Christians to the subject of faith and healing.

The Roots of Faith Formula Thinking

"Faith formula" thinking is based on the theory that there is a strict causality between faith and healing. It holds that all divine blessings, such as health and prosperity, are constantly and fully available to all Christians. These benefits, which are supposedly available to every and any child of God, may be instantly appropriated, provided the individual Christian knows enough and believes enough. The most dominant feature of this kind of thinking is its human-centeredness.

"Faith formula" defines faith as the human will to believe. The human ability to believe is the key which unlocks God's treasure chest of gifts. Centering on human responsibility, this kind of thinking is most frequently found among those who identify themselves as Arminians, though it is not confined to Arminians and not all Arminians succumb to it.

Charles Farah, a professor at Oral Roberts University, traces the roots of such thinking in America back to nineteenth-century evangelist Charles Finney:

This high view of man and his abilities, fanned by the "can-do" spirit of American Expansionism, supported by the secular doctrine of "manifest destiny," became an important link to present-day charismatic humanism.[1]

Thomas Smail, a Scottish theologian and spokesman for charismatic renewal, laments that the human-centered orientation of Arminius and Finney

is deeply engraved in modern Pentecostalism out of its background in Methodist holiness teaching. The baptism of the Spirit and our reception of His gifts is dependent upon our fulfillment of the conditions God lays down. If we know enough, repent enough, pray enough, at the end we shall have them, but if not, we shall not.[2]

While "faith formula" teaching arose out of classical Pentecostalism, most modern Pentecostals would reject it in the extreme form which I am presenting here. When this human-centered theology is applied to healing, we end up with this formula: "If you fulfill God's conditions by believing enough, God will heal. If you do not fulfill his conditions by believing enough, he will not." Charles Farah observes that those who are committed to this formula are hung on the horn of a cruel dilemma. In this scheme "failure to be healed must always come back to lack of faith."[3]

Pastoral Problems

Some time ago, my aunt discovered she had cancer. She quickly gathered about herself a group of "Spirit-filled" Christians to pray over her. These prayer warriors tolerated no negative thinking regarding my aunt's healing. They "confessed positively" and fearlessly spoke "the word of faith." Being fully persuaded that "confession brings possession," they "named and claimed" her complete and immediate healing. Some even said she was already healed despite the symptoms. The group received numerous prophecies and visions which assured them that healing was inevitable.

Shock and disbelief overtook this group of faithful intercessors when she finally died. They had genuinely and thoroughly believed they had fulfilled the conditions for healing. Because of their commitment to a "faith formula" approach to healing, some were left with guilt feelings, suspecting that they had not believed hard enough, while others who knew better were mad at God for betraying them. These two negative options were logically the only ones open to them. Some in the group became so demoralized that they retreated to a less challenging form of Christianity, which did not include praying for the sick. They feared that if they did not have enough faith for her healing, they would never have enough for anyone's healing.

If there was ever a question in my mind about the existence of an absolute cause-and-effect relationship between faith and healing, it was utterly and totally destroyed by the death of the British pastor, evangelist and writer, David Watson. I had regular contact with David during the years prior to his death. In addition to helping me in the founding of an evangelistic street mission, he inspired my interest in healing and deliverance. He was fully persuaded that God heals the sick today and claimed that God had on occasion healed him.

After David's cancer was diagnosed, many prayer meetings were called on his behalf all over the world. I personally participated in prayer for him in Canada, the United States and Holland. I have firsthand knowledge that he was prayed for expertly, faithfully and abundantly to the end. Along with Billy Graham and the Pope, David Watson may have been one of the most prayed-for religious leaders in recent history, and yet he died as the doctors predicted. I am sure that if enough prayer and faith guaranteed healing, David would be alive today.

Healing in the Absence of Faith

I have other, more positive, reasons for discounting an absolute causality between faith and healing. I can recall many instances of obvious and dramatic healings which have occurred in the absence of expectant faith. Some time ago, a young man we will call Mark came to my wife and me for marriage counseling. While playing football the day before he visited us, he tore the tendons on the outside of his left ankle. After an examination, which included X-rays, his swollen and terribly discolored lower leg and foot were placed in a cast.

As Patti and I prayed for his marriage, we prayed for his ankle as well. Mark came from a Christian tradition that held that healing, along with most other spiritual gifts, ceased with the apostles, and he only let us pray for him out of courtesy to us. Neither Patti nor I had any great faith that he would be healed, only that the pain might subside so that he could get back to work. The next day Mark accidentally stepped into a puddle of water and got his cast wet. When Mark went to the hospital to get his cast replaced the doctor cut it off and found no evidence of injury. There was a trace of discoloration but no swelling, and the new X-rays showed no damage to his tendons. That evening I watched Mark play volleyball!

On another occasion, as I was conducting a healing seminar, I got a strong impression that there was a woman present named Jan, who had skin cancer. I stated that I thought we were to pray for her. A woman named Jan, with skin cancer on her right cheek, came up to the front. Jan was from a very conservative Christian background that had instilled in her a deep distrust of anything vaguely miraculous. The healings which she had witnessed on this evening, prior to my calling her up, had not encouraged her but had deepened her fear. Only reluctantly did she let us pray for her, and when we finished, she seemed genuinely relieved that apparently nothing had happened. Jan returned the following evening to show us the place where the open, itching lesion had been the night before. There was now no trace of skin cancer. It had disappeared despite her lack of faith.

During the first months of my learning to pray for the sick, a youth in our neighborhood asked me for help. He was a local drug dealer and user and, though my wife and I frequently spoke to him about Jesus, he showed no interest. He asked for help because his arm got infected from a dirty needle. It was bright red, swollen and hot to the touch. He feared going to the hospital because of the questions which would inevitably be asked. Even though I did not expect God to respond under those circumstances, I said I could pray. So halfheartedly I asked God to help him. The result was dramatic. Within five minutes his arm was almost normal. I was unaware of anything even vaguely resembling faith in either of us.

Judging from such experiences, I find the connection between faith and healing is more mysterious and ambiguous than the "faith formula" teachers hold. The fact that this theory does not reflect everyday reality makes it suspect. Its often disastrous pastoral consequences make it dangerous.

Faith Formula and Guilt

A friend of mine lost her husband of forty years to a kidney disease. Following his death, she was haunted by the fear that her faltering faith during the last stages of his illness allowed him to die. Towards the end of his painful battle, she had on two or three occasions wished that it was over and that he could die in peace. After his death, she found her mind constantly returning to those moments of faltering faith, and she was plagued by guilt feelings. After counseling and reassurance from friends, she was delivered of anxiety which otherwise might have destroyed her.

One who was not so delivered of the guilt residue of "faith formula" teaching was a man who lost his five-year-old son to a blood disease. After the boy's death, the father suffered tremendous guilt because he believed his faith had not been strong enough to heal his son. Eight months later, the man himself died of a stress-induced disease.

While the "faith formula" fails the normal test of reality and too often proves pastorally disastrous, there are also biblical and theological reasons to regard it as a hindrance. The view of God which this teaching reflects bears little resemblance to the God of the Bible. The god of "faith formula" thinking can heal sickness but awaits some specific quality and quantity of faith to be offered up to him before healing is released. This god's relationship with his people seems more contractual than covenantal. He requires a certain amount of human faith/work before releasing his blessings. If blessings are not released, it is because the work has not been done. In my opinion, this largely accounts for the volume of noise and emotionalism at some healing meetings. The frenzy is a form of work, which people believe will get God moving. God, they think, responds to his people because of their work rather than because of his grace.

In "faith formula" teaching, there is great emphasis on "claiming the promises" and the almost magical power of "positive confession." It is taught that if you know how to "write your own ticket with God,"[4] you will get results from prayer. The clear impression is that enough of the right kind of human effort can get God to do almost anything. This is not unlike the Babylonian belief in fertility gods. The Babylonians believed the gods would act if enough of the right offering was made in the proper fashion. Any view of prayer that subordinates the acts of God to the offerings of his creatures, even the offering of "faith," is contrary to biblical teaching. It is true that God has promised us blessings and we may expect them, but we are never told to claim them.

"Faith formula" teaching not only disfigures God, but also distorts the realities of our present life as taught in Scripture. Exponents of "faith formula" theology display a naive belief that the kingdom of God has fully come, here and now. There seems to be little understanding of the partial and provisional nature of the king-dom of God this side of the Second Coming of Christ. "Faith for-mula" teachers have little tolerance of suffering of any kind. They believe that a full realization of kingdom blessings is prevented only by our lack of faith. Paul, however, assures us that if we are to share in the kingdom blessings in the future, we must share Christ's suf-fering now (Rom 8:17). This is why Paul rejoices in his sufferings (Col 1:24).

In Scripture God has clearly promised to comfort and vindicate his own. He has, however, seldom promised to do so immediately. In Hebrews 11:32-39, we find those who by faith won great victo-ries while others by faith suffered and died. Immediate vindication and total victory were not promised to the Hebrews; they have been saved for the end of the age (10:35-36).

The Proper Role of Faith

In remaining faithful to his Pentecostal roots yet sharply criticizing "faith formula" thinking, Gordon Fee states:

> God is revealed to have limitless power and resources; He reg-ularly shows Himself strong on behalf of His people. Yet His people still live out their redeemed lives in a fallen world, where the whole creation, including the human body, is in "bondage to decay" (Rom 8:21), and will continue to be so until we receive "the redemption of our bodies" (8:23).[5]

Here Fee directs us to Romans 8 where Paul presents to us this already-and-not-yet character of Christian life and ministry. Paul begins with this unambiguous declaration: "Therefore, there is now no condemnation for those who are in Christ Jesus" (v. 1). The security and power of our reconciliation is now objectively absolute. At the same time, our not-yet subjective reality is characterized by inner groanings "as we wait eagerly for our adoption as sons, the redemption of our bodies" (v. 23). We live in the manifest power of God's healing today as we await the consummation of that reality tomorrow. Maturity in Christian life and ministry requires that we do so gracefully. The Christian believes that not only today but also tomorrow belongs to God. This is why Thomas Smail counsels:

> When the prayer made in faith is not answered and the healing for which many have sought does not come, we are not to look for someone to accuse of failure in faith. Rather we are to remember that besides faith there is hope. Hope has to do with God's promises that are still future and hidden, just as faith has to do with God's promises that are here and now. To the person who has believed for today but has not seen the answer come today, there comes the call to hope. Hope says, "Tomorrow also is God's. Enough has happened already to assure you that the rest is on the way."[6]

And not only should the sufferer be assured of God's deliverance in the future, but also of his steadfast love in the present. Paul asserts, "Neither death nor life, neither angels nor demons, neither the present nor the future, nor any powers, neither height nor depth, nor anything else in all creation, will be able to separate us from the love of God" (Rom 8:38-39).

God's power is as near to us in sickness and in death as it is in healing. The one who prays, yet is not healed, need never question that reality. The biblically informed follower of Jesus Christ knows how to trust God for physical as well as spiritual healing and knows how to persist in trusting God when the effects of a fallen world continue to be with us. Any gospel of healing which cannot be spoken with confidence and received as comfort at the deathbed is not the gospel of Jesus Christ.

One of the weakest elements in "faith formula" teaching is its view of the biblical function of faith. "Faith formula" holds that the function of faith is to get results. Faith is assumed to precede and produce miracles. In many New Testament instances faith in Jesus did precede healings (Mt 8:10; 9:18; 14:31; Mk 2:4; 5:36; Lk 7:50; 17:6). In other instances, however, miracles preceded and served to produce faith (Mt 11:4; Lk 24:13-35; Jn 9:1-38; 10:37; 12:37; 20:31).

One of the most damaging effects of "faith formula" thinking is that many Christians falsely equate it with the Christian healing ministry in general. A significant number of evangelical believers are deeply prejudiced against "healers" of any style because of the highly visible and influential "faith formula" healers of the past and present. The fear of the "fringe" elements in the body of Christ is used as an excuse to steer clear of the entire issue of healing. Those of us from Catholic, Anglican, Pentecostal or mainstream evangelical traditions are often thought to hold the same beliefs as "faith formula" evangelists simply because we pray for the sick and train others in this ministry. This is all the more reason to isolate this kind of thinking and to root it out.

I hasten to add that in so doing I do not wish to declare guilty by association all Pentecostals and charismatics. Most Pentecostals and charismatics, like Charles Farah, Thomas Smail and Gordon Fee, are only too aware of the errors of "faith formula" teaching.

Let me also confess my personal indebtedness to Pentecostals and charismatic healers of the past and present. I believe that the body of Christ in general is stronger today because they were willing to believe God's promises when most were not and because they took risks based on those promises when most did not. My sincere desire today is to be helped by and to be of help to those from any Christian tradition who, in the name of the Lord Jesus Christ, seek to participate in his ministry of healing, deliverance and reconciliation.

And in defense specifically of "faith formula" teachers, let me say that while I believe that they exaggerate what is fully available to us now, they are still closer to the truth than those who deny the availability of healing now.

In summing up our discussion thus far of the various theological hindrances to a healing ministry, we have seen that embracing sickness as a sanctifying blessing, passively accepting illness as a decree of God, and substituting presumption for genuine faith all distort the biblical view of sickness and healing. Identifying and isolating these hindrances clears the ground for a discussion of the scriptural view of healing; however, another major obstruction remains. That obstruction is the world view which supports even Christian skepticism about healing.

CHAPTER FOUR

THE SECULAR WORLD VIEW

LIKE THE FIRST-CENTURY WORLD OF THE NEW TESTAMENT, most non-Western cultures today are open to the possibility of supernatural healing. Their world view allows for the miraculous. The modern secular world view, which most of us in Europe, Australia, New Zealand, South Africa, Canada and the United States share, denies the possibility of miracles. For this reason, supernatural healing is generally not anticipated or accepted by our culture—though, oddly enough, people in many Western countries, particularly Germany, France and Austria, are turning for "healing" to spiritualists and other occult practitioners. Christian healing, however, is rare. The theologian Don Cupitt explains what I mean:

In the present century modern man has come into a new kind of understanding of himself and his place in the universe which has

made obsolete all previous world views . . . so we have come by
now to a completely secular view of the world and our place in
it.[1]

Secularism is that system of thought that denies the existence or
significance of anything religious. God is removed from the modern
view of reality so the world is now understood to be a closed system,
governed by the cause and effect of natural laws. These laws are
discovered by scientifically observing the empirical world. Thus as
David Hume says:

A miracle is a violation of the laws of nature . . . a firm and
unalterable experience has established these laws, the proof
against a miracle, from the very nature of the fact, is as entire as
any argument from experience can possibly be imagined.[2]

Modern scientific materialists along with Hume are asking, "Hasn't
science proved that the universe is closed and mechanistic thus making God passé? Are not all human experiences explainable in terms
of natural processes therefore eliminating any need for the supernatural?"

We moderns tend to function mostly without reference to God.
Thus we are oriented almost exclusively to the secular. My premise
in this book—that "power from on high" is manifest as servants of
the Most High pray—is ruled out from the start by a secular world
view. Unless we make a conscious effort to resist the view of reality
we are born into and conditioned by, there is little chance we will
with any confidence pray for the sick and see them healed.

Every culture has a distinct world view, although few of us can
identify our own or articulate it. One reason for this is that each of
us believes our own view of the world is the way it really is. It rarely
occurs to us that our point of view is just one among many possible
points of view. None of us choose our world view any more than
we choose our mother tongue. We are born to it and to a significant
degree conditioned by it forever after. World views are internalized
beliefs about reality and generally go unquestioned throughout life.

This is why the secular world view is not so much a weed which chokes out good seed, but rather the polluted ground in which the seed is planted. Our view of reality is not skewed by one particular erroneous thought but by a whole system of thought. Gaining some perspective on the modern world view is the first step towards being able to resist it.[3]

The Development of the Modern Mind

The secular world view is a relatively recent development in world history. Prior to the 1600s, all views of the world were theistic. The categories of thought in every known culture were rooted in the belief that the God or the gods were real and somehow present and active in the world. Then in the midseventeenth century the work of René Descartes began to change the status quo in Europe.

Descartes developed a view of the world based on mathematics.[4] He believed and taught that all reality resulted from mechanical cause and effect and that it could be conceptualized mathematically. Though Descartes himself believed in God—indeed he believed that it was impossible for God not to exist—he nevertheless started a trend in philosophy that soon led to the exclusion of God from philosophical accounts of reality. For Descartes, God was a starting point, an assumption that guaranteed that the rest of his system would hold up, but God had no further role in the system. Other philosophers soon found little reason to include God at the start.

Gradually the theological view of reality was replaced by a scientific, mechanistic view. Instead of thinking of the world and its history in relationship to God, people began to think of it as an autonomous machine. The agenda of science was no longer to "think God's thoughts after him" but to discover the laws which govern the universe. It was believed that as these laws were discovered, the movements of the "machine" could be predicted and eventually controlled. Modern technology shows clearly how successful this program has been. The result is that, for the most part, people today find God rather unnecessary.

This shift in our world view is a revolution of the first order. As Roman Catholic theologian Malachi Martin puts it:

> Almost one hundred years ago, Western culture in Europe and the United States underwent its one and only radical religious change since the fourth century.... That change, apparent among Europeans and Americans by the 1800s, was an utterly new thing: unbelief in God as an acceptable option.[5]

This is not to say that none of us believe in God anymore, but rather that he has become nonessential to the way we live our lives. We Western Christians may be theists in our heads, but we tend to act like secularists in our daily activities. The real authority in our world view today and the touchstone of truth for our society is science. Science is our savior, provider and fixer.

Virtually every policy of social life, government and education, as well as people's personal philosophies of life, are evaluated in terms of their being scientific or unscientific. It is generally believed that for a thing to be true, it must be scientifically proven. Truth has become more or less synonymous with that which can be scientifically established. Nonmaterialistic values—like love, justice and religion—which cannot be scientifically proven are regarded as either irrelevant or simply a matter of preference.

The Scientific View of Healing

Understandably, our scientifically controlled world view has profoundly affected modern health care. Today it is not God but medical science which is looked to for healing. The British health expert Thomas McKlown says this about our view of sickness and healing and how we came by it:

> The approach to biology and medicine established during the seventeenth century was an engineering one based on a physical model. Nature was conceived in mechanistic terms, which led biology to the idea that an organism could be regarded as a

> machine which might be taken apart and reassembled if its structure and function were fully understood.[6]

The belief that the human organism is only matter in motion, plus our skepticism regarding the reality and relevance of the spiritual world, makes praying for the sick a rare occurrence in the Western world. When we do pray, we do so with little assurance. And when someone is healed as a result of prayer, we may not recognize it as such.

Two years ago, a twenty-six-year-old woman approached my wife and me for prayer. Liz told us that since the age of six she had suffered from epileptic seizures. For the past twenty years she had been treated with drugs which largely, but not entirely, controlled her symptoms. In addition to her brain disturbance, she suffered severe migraine headaches, which no amount of medication relieved. The headaches became so bad that she had missed months of school, and they made holding down a steady job impossible.

We prayed twice for Liz with no apparent effect. When she came the third time she was suffering from headache pain. As we prayed this time, the pain lifted and in that instant she felt something "shift" within her body. She later told us that the "shift" she felt was the departure of an unclean spirit.

Liz was due for her next six-month checkup the following week. This examination included an EEG which monitored her brain activity. This test showed no sign of disturbance, and her doctors assumed that there was a malfunction in the machine and scheduled another test. The second exam also showed no sign of the previous illness, so her medication was reduced by one-half. Two weeks later the doctors examined her again, and still there was no evidence of epilepsy. She then discontinued her medication altogether. Two years have now passed, and she still has no symptoms of epilepsy, nor has she had any recurrence of migraine headaches.

Her doctors are pleased but puzzled. They have found it impossible to accept her testimony that God healed her through prayer.

Their Western world view has ruled out the possibility of divine intervention. In an attempt to account for Liz's present health, they have concluded that she must have been misdiagnosed and mistreated for the past twenty years. These conscientious and competent doctors have risked a possible malpractice suit rather than admit the possibility of divine healing.

Our modern blindness to God's hand in healing sometimes has serious consequences. As my team and I were praying for the sick one Saturday morning, a woman I will call Brenda came for help. She had been told by her doctor the previous Thursday that the pain and the bleeding she was experiencing were caused by cancer in her uterus. X-rays, a physical exam and a biopsy all confirmed that her womb, which was full of cancer, had to be removed immediately. She was scheduled for surgery the following Tuesday.

As we spoke to her and prayed for her, we all sensed that the power to heal was with us. Brenda believed that something had happened to her and so decided to ask her doctors for additional tests to check for improvement. If she could avoid the surgery, she definitely wished to.

Because of the life-threatening nature of her disease and because divine healing was not considered a possibility, her doctors pressed her not to get more tests but to have the operation as scheduled. She consented and underwent surgery.

After her uterus was removed, it was examined by the doctors who performed the operation. To the surprise of everyone, no trace of cancer was found except some scarring. The uterus which had been full of cancer five days prior was now clean and had been unnecessarily removed. Though Brenda's doctors have no explanation themselves, they are not considering the possibility that God healed her. C. S. Lewis once pointed out that for many moderns seeing is not believing.

This is the first thing to get clear in talking about miracles. Whatever experiences we may have, we shall not regard them as mi-

raculous if we already hold a philosophy which excludes the supernatural.[7]

The perceived "scientific" impossibility of power from on high af-
fecting the body and mind of individuals makes "medical verifica-
tion" problematic. Divine healing does occur, but a system of
thought controlled by the secular world view does not perceive it
as such.

Fortunately this is changing as more and more doctors and psy-
chiatrists who have respect for Scripture begin to take their belief
in the Bible as seriously as they have taken their medical training.
Many Christian healing communities now have doctors and other
trained professionals consulting and praying with those who minister to the sick and demonized.

My judgment is that the combination of loving prayer with medical and psychological expertise creates the optimum conditions for
healing to occur. I have found the guidance, support and fellowship
of Christian doctors and counselors to be invaluable. I understand
medical science to be a gift of God to his creatures. Along with
prayer, this gift is given to us to aid in combating the effects of sin
in the world. My wife and our fourth son would not be alive today
were it not for a skilled surgeon. Medical science and Christian faith
fight a common enemy with different means; therefore the polarization between science and faith is false. What God has joined together must not be torn apart.

The real tension is not between church and science but between
a secular world view and a view of reality which allows for the
activity of the living God. In fact, the church all too often seems to
agree with the world's skepticism about the possibility of God's
acting in the world. Evangelical biblical scholars are generally em-
barrassed by biblical miracles. Despite the fact that over one-third
of the Synoptic Gospels deals with some form of the miraculous,
miracles are rarely seriously discussed by them. Donald Guthrie, for
instance, in his massive and otherwise comprehensive and conserva-

tive treatment of New Testament theology, gives no attention to miracles whatever.

In general, the church in the West functions more or less like other secular institutions—we rely on human effort. If we set goals at all, they tend to be "realistic." In the main, we act as if we do not anticipate power from on high breaking into our programs and significantly altering their effectiveness. For the most part, we have accommodated church life to secular powerlessness and predictability. While we try to resist secularism at an intellectual level, we lose ground to it in practice. We say to the world that we are sent to it in the name of the omnipotent God of creation, yet we often stand helpless before situations which desperately need his power. Not just disobedience but our world view is to blame for this condition.

Miracles and Expectation
Christian communities in other parts of the world that do not share our world view do not share our powerlessness either. Churches in Africa, Asia and South America, where Western thinking does not predominate, experience the reality of Paul's words to the Corinthians that "the kingdom of God is not a matter of talk but of power" (1 Cor 4:20).

My friend John White recently told our Sunday morning congregation an interesting story about miracles and world views. Three years ago he and his wife, Lorrie, went on an extensive preaching tour of Asia and the South Seas. They began in Japan, China and Malaysia. In each of these countries they preached the gospel and prayed for the sick. Frequently people in these countries were healed as a result—some dramatically. When they arrived in Australia, the last leg of their trip, the healings and miracles stopped abruptly. The world view which John and Lorrie found in Asia accepted the healings for which they prayed; the world view in Australia did not.

Where people do not expect miracles, they rarely see them; and where they do expect God's power to be at work, they often see it.

Western missiologists Peter Wagner, Paul Kaufman and Charles Kraft assure us that miracles of healing, as well as other signs and wonders, are commonplace in many Third World churches. Where this is the case, effective evangelism and rapid church growth usually follow.

Some seminaries are now beginning to help missionaries and pastors compensate for their Western world view by giving them training in praying for the sick and demonized. I know from personal experience, having taken one of these courses, that our world view can be stretched significantly.

I do not mean to suggest that a shift in world view comes easily or can ever be complete. The intellectual environment in which we have been raised will always be a part of us. After many hours of theological reflection and after having seen hundreds of people healed of sickness and delivered of evil spirits, I still find in myself a fibrous root of skepticism. For me to pray for the sick demands a conscious and consistent recommitment to the Bible and its view of reality. For modern Christians this daily recommitment to the biblical world view is a practical application of Paul's exhortation: "Do not conform any longer to the pattern of this world, but be transformed by the renewing of your mind" (Rom 12:2).

A strong element in "the pattern of this world" to which we are not to conform is the modern scientific demand for incontrovertible clinical proof. Specifically we ought not to demand proof that Jesus miraculously heals the sick today before we are willing to pray. We are to "renew our minds" by first suspending our scientific skepticism about miracles and then beginning to pray for the sick to be healed.

But not only is trusting and acting on Christ's character demanded of us, without it we will not see the glory of Christ revealed in his healing ministry. The skeptical Pharisees in Matthew 16:1-4 demanded a "sign from heaven," incontrovertible proof that Jesus was who he claimed to be. Jesus refused flatly. The next event recorded in Matthew 16 is Peter's confession of faith in Christ (vv. 15-16), followed by the transfiguration (Mt 17:1-7)—a "sign from heaven," which was incontrovertible proof that Jesus was who he claimed to be. Note the order of these events: first faith, then a "sign from heaven." The glory of God revealed in healing is not given to skeptics in order to persuade them; instead it is given to those who trust the Lord and act on his Word.

Modern skeptics demand proof of healing before they believe in it. I used to accommodate these demands by collecting testimonies and medical reports to offer as proof. My efforts, however, were in vain because modern day Pharisees, Christian and pagan, seem never to be persuaded by evidence even when it is clear and unambiguous. Jesus heals the sick, and his glory in doing so is revealed to those who renew their minds through believing in him and acting on his Word.

The renewing of our minds also involves the theological weeding we have done in this section. With the ground of our thinking somewhat cleared, we can more readily receive and nurture the Good Seed Jesus Christ. As we do, we will see that health is to be preferred to sickness, contrary to the values of "sanctification through sickness"; that healing is a possibility for all, not just a predestined few as "divine determinism" asserts; and that this possibility is rooted in the free sovereign love of God, not in human effort as "faith formula" holds. And then we will have one more reason to rejoice in the truth that the gospel of Jesus Christ is indeed good news.

As Leslie D. Weatherhead says,

Man should part forever with the idea that sickness or disease is the inscrutable will of God, that he sends it in order to discipline man, and that resignation is the attitude required of us. God created the body to be the perfect instrument of the Spirit. It cannot be his will that it should function imperfectly.[8]

It may well be that the whole fellowship of the church needs to be raised to a higher spiritual level today before individual healers in it can repeat the healing activities of the Son of God, and that until the groups within the church today are willing to pass through the same kind of discipline, the healing ministry of the church will be restricted.[9]

PART II

THE KINGDOM OF GOD
AND THE FIGHT TO HEAL

MOST OF US HAVE JOINED THE BIBLICAL WRITERS in concluding that something has gone very wrong with the world and with each of us individually. David laments our condition like this: "Surely I was sinful at birth, sinful from the time my mother conceived me" (Ps 51:5). David realized not only that he did wrong but that something had been seriously wrong with him from the beginning.

The Bible teaches that this essential wrongness at the core of human history and the human soul resulted from sin and is exploited by Satan. The first man, Adam, was the first sinner. By rebelling against God, the true king of all the earth, Adam delivered himself and his descendants into the hands of Satan who became the false king of all the earth. Because of Adam's original sin we are all born into the service of Satan. We are all subjects of his pseudokingdom which has become the comprehensive counterfeit or negative image of the world God created.

Sickness in all its expressions is characteristic of Satan's pseudo-kingdom. As Michael Green states:

> Disease and death are all part and parcel of the spurious deal the devil gave in return for primal man's "Yes" to temptation. In some mysterious way sin, disease and death are all part of the heritage of disobedience.[1]

Through the disobedience of the first Adam, the world and its inhabitants were subjected to Satan's oppression. Through the obedience of Christ, the last Adam, the world and its inhabitants have been rescued out of Satan's pseudokingdom into the kingdom of God. The kingdom of God revealed in Jesus brings comprehensive healing to all that sin and Satan have wounded. Jesus did more than save our souls, he saved all that we are. Salvation through Jesus Christ is not just a legal justification before God—it is a concrete, historical rescue and healing. In this rescue and healing we are saved from the wrongness at the core of human history and the human soul.

Lutheran theologian James Kallas explains:

> If we see the work of Jesus as the defeat of Satan and the destruction of Satan's grip on this world, then suddenly the life, work, death, resurrection of Jesus assumes an impressive unity. He begins the fight with Satan in the exorcisms and healings, attacks Satan where he is strongest . . . in the realm of death by bringing them back to life . . . and then Himself shatters death as the ultimate weapon of Satan, thus completely destroying the power of Satan. The life of Jesus thus seen is a cohesive, closely knit ascending battle which reaches its climax in the resurrection.[2]

The resurrection was the decisive victory for the kingdom of God, yet for a season Satan retains significant power expressed in physical and mental disease and spiritual bondage. Although Jesus dealt the

Devil and his pseudokingdom a deathblow on the cross, Satan does not yield his dark realm gracefully to the rule of the kingdom of God. The victory of God's kingdom over Satan will not be complete till the return of Jesus Christ. The cosmic battle between the forces of darkness and light is real. There are victories and losses on both sides. Part of the church's assignment in this real fight is "to preach the kingdom of God and to heal the sick" (Lk 9:2). Jesus' command to preach the kingdom of God and to heal the sick is more than an outline of the mission of the church, it reflects the will of his Father in heaven, specifically his Father's will regarding sickness and healing.

CHAPTER FIVE

GOD DESIRES TO HEAL THE SICK

GOD WILLS THE ULTIMATE HEALING OF ALL SPIRITUAL, PSY-chological and physical sickness. This complete healing comes to us through the atonement arising from the death and resurrection of Jesus Christ. We receive this final, comprehensive healing at our resurrection from the dead. So too, as a sign and seal of this prom-ise, God often sends healing today. The healing of an illness and the grace to endure in hope when healing is delayed is the reality of God standing with us now. God upholds us in our fight against sickness because as J. I. Packer says:

> God's love to sinners involves His *identifying Himself with their welfare*. Such an identification is involved in all love: it is, indeed, the test of whether love is genuine or not. . . . It is not for noth-ing that the Bible habitually speaks of God as the loving Father

and Husband of His people. It follows from the very nature of these relationships that God's happiness will not be complete till all His beloved ones are finally out of trouble: . . . He has in effect resolved that henceforth for all eternity His happiness shall be conditional upon ours. Thus God saves, not only for His glory, but for His gladness.[1]

The more secure we are in the belief that God wills our health and that he personally works for it, the more freely we receive his healing and the more eagerly we work for it in others. Openly receiving healing for ourselves and confidently praying for others rests ultimately in our understanding of who God is. In any issue relating to God, the *who* question is prior to all others. If we believe that God is the one who is not happy "till all His beloved ones are finally out of trouble," as J. I. Packer asserts, then we may expect him to desire our healing. Some of us do not, however, expect God to desire our healing because we see him differently than Packer and the Bible portray him.

Distorted Views of Healing

Erroneous views of healing arise out of erroneous views of God. The Greeks, for instance, saw God as essentially removed from human beings and uninterested in their welfare. They regarded the body as evil, the spirit as good, and therefore a relationship between the two as impossible. This dualism between the human and the divine worlds made it unthinkable for the Deity to be moved by human suffering or to act on behalf of the sufferer. It is not difficult to see why the Greeks did not develop a doctrine of divine healing.

The Islamic view of God rules out the possibility of a theology of healing for different reasons. Islam teaches that God has decreed blessing for some and pain for others and that nothing we do may alter these circumstances. This *kismet* or fate determining health for some and sickness for others makes the thought of praying for the sick ludicrous.

A theology of healing arises only when God is viewed as one who is concerned about sickness and willing to do something about it. Biblical Christians confess faith in just such a God. We say that our knowledge of God is derived from Scripture generally and revealed in Jesus Christ specifically. We believe that God was in Christ, that the will of God was done through Christ.

If this is true, why then are so many of our theological assertions about sickness and healing inconsistent with this perspective? As we passively accept sickness as God's will or embrace it as his blessing, we contradict what we say we believe about the character of God revealed in Christ. Either we fail logically to connect what we say about sickness and healing to what we believe about God, or we do not really believe about God what we claim.

The early church fathers asserted that Jesus is of one essence and being with the Father. They saw that if Jesus is different in essence from God the Father, then we do not know God. Or as Jesus put it in Matthew 11:27, "No one knows the Father except the Son and those to whom the Son chooses to reveal him."

A teacher in the early church, named Arius, expounded the view that while Jesus was a unique "son of God," he was not the same essence as God. As a Greek thinker, he believed that true deity does not come into contact with the physical world. So the man Jesus could not be one with God, though he was an agent of God.

The Greek father Athanasius saw that if this doctrine of God was believed, then any theology which arose from it would of necessity be in error. If Jesus is not God, then we can do little more than speculate about the character of God. And so if Jesus is not God, then we can do little more than speculate about his willingness to heal. But, as the church fathers and evangelical theology assert, if we have seen Jesus, we have seen the Father. Jesus the man may not have disclosed all of God, but that which was disclosed is accurate, trustworthy and eternally true. God's self-revelation through human flesh may be indirect, but it is not inaccurate.

Before we hasten to affirm this, let us recognize that we do not always act as if we believe it. Or if we believe it, we have not consistently applied it to the rest of our theology, particularly our theology of sickness and healing.

I say this because we so often seem to see Jesus and God as different beings. Many of us regard Jesus as the loving and forgiving side of God and the Father as the more stern and demanding side of God. It is as if Jesus is perceived as the friendly face of God revealed on the stage of human history and the Father as the not-so-friendly face concealed offstage in the shadows. For many of us Jesus seems too loving, too forgiving, too liberal for the Father.

When we suspect that God wills sickness and entertain doubts about his desire to heal it, we betray that what we think about the character of God is not rooted in the revelation of God in Christ but arises from the shadows somewhere offstage. But if Jesus truly reveals the character of God to us, then we may cease speculating about and arguing over God's will in sickness and healing. His attitude in these matters is clearly set down on the pages of the New Testament.

Jesus Reveals God's Heart

Just as the Old Testament writers before them, the New Testament writers understood God, not through speculation, but through his concrete acts in history, and now supremely through the life, death and resurrection of Jesus. "In the past God spoke to our forefathers through the prophets . . . but in these last days he has spoken to us by his Son" (Heb 1:1-2). Or as the evangelical theologian Thomas Torrance says:

> Incarnate as a Jew from Bethlehem and Nazareth Jesus stood forth . . . as . . . the personal self-revelation of God to man. . . . What God the Father has revealed of Himself in Jesus Christ, His Son, He is in Himself.[2]

That is to say, all that God was communicating through the Law and the Prophets is now focused in Christ. Jesus as the self-revelation of the Father is the inner meaning of all that God has been saying about himself throughout history. Jesus has become the horizon of our knowledge of God. We need no longer speculate about God's character. God himself has disclosed his character and made clear his attitudes towards us in his Son, the Lord Jesus Christ.

The Gospel writers were aware that they were recording for others the revelation of God in the words and deeds of Jesus. An example of this is found in John 1. Here the author speaks of Jesus as the *Logos*—as the Word of God who reveals the being of God. In verse eighteen, he states, "No one has ever seen God, but God the One and Only, who is at the Father's side, has made him known." The Greek word for "has made known" is the word from which we get the English word *exegesis*. That is to say, Jesus is the only exegesis of God. He alone explains the character and being of God. He uniquely reveals the inner life of the Father. Jesus is as essential to God's self-communication as words are to our self-communication. A revelation of the Father without the Son would be like speaking without words.

In commenting on John 1:18, Leon Morris explains, "Jesus has now given full account of the Father."[3] Stephen Neill adds the following qualification, "God may be inscrutable; but if He is really God, there can be nothing to prevent Him from making known everything of Himself that can be known by man. And this is exactly what He has done."[4]

Jesus himself said, "The Son can do nothing by himself; he can do only what he sees his Father doing, because whatever the Father does the Son also does" (Jn 5:19). Thus Jesus is not only dependent on the Father's will but also faithful in accurately revealing it. It is in this light that we should view Jesus' healing miracles. They reveal something essential about the character of the Father, in particular, his consistent and unambiguous hostility towards sickness and his desire to heal it.

From this point forward we will avoid any discussion of theories about healing which have accumulated in our traditions and turn instead to what God himself, in Christ, discloses on the subject. As we do, we will find cause for great joy. Jesus reveals that God is concerned even for our relatively trivial pains. The shortage of wine at Cana, for instance, was little more than an embarrassment, yet Jesus attended to it (Jn 2:1-11). The hungry multitudes in Matthew 15 were not starving, but Jesus gladly fed them.

In more important matters, Jesus revealed that God is so concerned to heal our sicknesses that he may not even take into account the sins which caused them. Karl Barth explains that the important thing about the people in Jesus' miracle stories is not that they were sinners, even though they were, but that they were sufferers:

> Jesus does not just look at their past, and then at their tragic present in light of it. But from their present He creates for them a new future. He does not ask, therefore, concerning their sin. He does not hold it against them. He does not denounce them because of it. The help and blessing He brings are quite irrespective of the sin. He acts exactly in the same way as His Father in heaven, who causes His sun to shine on the good and evil, His rain to fall on the just and the unjust.[5]

Jesus acts exactly as his Father in heaven acts. He does only what he sees the Father doing. As he does, he shows us that God indeed wills to heal the sick. A major element in his willingness to heal the sick is his compassion.

> On every page of [Luke's] Gospel is apparent the deep sympathy of Jesus for men and women, with their wrecked lives, their physical and mental sufferings, their heart-rending sorrows, the tragedy of their sins. Not less apparent is His determination to right their lot.[6]

The Heritage of an Emotionless God
Some may not think of God as being emotional, but as biblical

commentator Hugh Martin points out, he is deeply feeling and caring. God's attitude towards us and his activity in history are not rooted merely in divine wisdom and will, but spring from an emotional life, deep within his being.

Among the elements in traditional theology which have deterred us from praying effectively for the sick is the all-too-common notion that God is emotionally removed from our suffering. As philosopher and theologian Charles Hartshorne explains:

Throughout the Christian centuries there have been few theologians who have rejected the conception of God as pure intellect or will, as knowing our feelings but feeling nothing, willing our good but not in any intelligible sense caring about our pleasures or sufferings. Most theologians rejected feeling as a divine attribute. For them it connoted weakness.[7]

The idea that God is aloof from what we call feelings is part of the divine attribute labeled "impassibility" in standard theology texts. This technical term simply means "unable to be moved, incapable of suffering injury or pain." This conception derives more from Greek philosophy than from biblical revelation.

The Greeks reasoned that if God could be moved at all by any pleasure or pain, it would imply he was unstable or incomplete. They did not think of God as a person as such, but as the absolute perfection of beauty and truth. Any movement from that pinnacle of perfection would have been understood as a move towards imperfection. Thus the possibility of divine emotion was ruled out. Unfortunately, Christian theology followed Greek metaphysics here.

Despite the conflict between this understanding of God and the numerous biblical references to God's emotions—his anger, joy and compassion—most Protestants as well as Catholics even today have inherited this view of God in one form or another. The result is often plain in our attempts to intercede for a family member who is in some trouble. Our prayers take the form of a legal argument—"Lord, if anyone deserves healing it surely is Mary." This implies that God doesn't care about Mary but may respond to the need if it is presented in the form of a legal brief.

On other occasions, the tone of our intercessions degenerates to begging and bargaining. Inherent in this is the tacit belief that God really does not feel or care for those in trouble. Though he sheds no tears, we think he may be prompted to act by ours.

Then, too, we hear about intercessory prayer as the "storming of the gates of heaven." This conjures up the notion that God is locked behind doors of brass and will only take notice of us if we clamor hard enough and long enough. I believe that our praying may be emotional and that it should be persistent, yet the anxiety which characterizes much of our praying is rooted in this wrong view of God's emotional life.

Jesus' Compassion

The Bible teaches that God was in Christ, and therefore he not only cares deeply about our pain but also has experienced it. God was fully present in the flesh of Jesus of Nazareth as that flesh suffered hunger, thirst, weariness and as it was pierced and torn on the cross of Golgotha. He not only is concerned about the pain caused by the world's sin, he has personally experienced that pain.

The Gospels record God's identification with us in all types of suffering and also show his resolve to heal that suffering. In the New Testament we find a Greek word for compassion (*splanchnizomai*) that gives exquisite testimony to God's caring for our pain and to his determination to alleviate it. The word stems from the word for "bowels" or "viscera" and often denotes the intestines of a sacrificial animal. In Hebrew a similar relationship exists between words that express the intense feelings of close natural bonds, such as that of mothers for their children, and words that refer to the belly or womb.

The kind of compassion Jesus had for people was not merely an expression of his will, but an eruption from deep within his being.

The word used to describe his compassion expresses the involuntary gasp wrenched from a man overwhelmed by a great sorrow or the groan of a woman savaged by labor pains. Out of this deep compassion sprang Jesus' mighty works of rescue, healing and deliverance. "When Jesus landed and saw a large crowd, he had compassion on them and healed their sick" (Mt 14:14).

Like a good shepherd Jesus was concerned for the total welfare of his people:

> Jesus went through all the towns and villages, teaching in their synagogues, preaching the good news of the kingdom and healing every disease and sickness. When he saw the crowds, he had compassion on them, because they were harassed and helpless, like sheep without a shepherd. (Mt 9:35-36)

In this passage, we see clearly the characteristic combining of Jesus' preaching and healing arising from his heart's compassion. Likewise, Jesus is moved at the sight of a crowd without food.

> Since they had nothing to eat, Jesus called his disciples to him and said, "I have compassion for these people; they have already been with me three days and have nothing to eat." (Mk 8:1-2)

The God who was in Christ is profoundly moved at the sight of his people deprived of spiritual or material food.

In Jesus' day, a woman alone without a man to care for her was in serious trouble. In Luke 7:13, Jesus came across just such a woman, a widow who was in the process of burying her only son. Jesus, moved with compassion for her in her social and physical vulnerability, raises her son to life again.

In Mark 1:40-41, we find a man who embodies all the physical, social and spiritual disintegration of a sinful world. At this sight, Jesus is overwrought with compassion.

> A man with leprosy came to him and begged him on his knees, "If you are willing, you can make me clean." Filled with compassion, Jesus reached out his hand and touched the man. "I am willing," he said. "Be clean!"

This intensely emotive language describing Jesus (and therefore God) is not peculiar to the Gospel writers. The entire New Testament witnesses to the truth that God's heart is moved for us and his power is near to us in our distress. "The Spirit himself," writes Paul, "intercedes for us with groans that words cannot express" (Rom 8:26).

When reflecting on the healing miracles of Christ, commentators are prone to regard them as means to ends. They see the miracles authenticating Jesus' divine Sonship or revealing the presence of the kingdom of God or as a way to do evangelism. While Jesus' miracles were effective means to these ends, they were also ends in themselves. The Gospel writers state that Jesus healed people because he loved them. Very simply, he had compassion for them; he was on their side; he wanted to solve their problems.

God himself is distressed by our plight, and his emotional response is powerful. Mighty acts of rescue, healing and deliverance flow from his compassion.

In commenting on the prophets, the Jewish theologian Abraham Heschel draws attention to the intense way the man or woman of God learns to identify with God's compassion:

> The pathos of God is on the prophet. It moves him. It breaks out in him like a storm in the soul, overwhelming his inner life, his thoughts, feelings, wishes and hopes. It takes possession of his heart, giving him courage to act.[8]

Just so may the compassion of God revealed in Christ take possession of our hearts, giving us courage to act on behalf of the sick all about us.

The healing ministry of Christ and his church, which is rooted in compassion, is not, however, simply a response to God's kindness but also an evidence of the advance of his kingdom. We turn to this next.

CHAPTER SIX

THE ASSAULT OF THE KINGDOM
OF GOD

MOST NEW TESTAMENT SCHOLARS AGREE THAT JESUS' CEN-
tral message concerned the kingdom of God. Jesus entrusted this
same message to the twelve apostles (Mt 10:7) and to the band of
seventy-two (Lk 10:9). It may seem surprising in light of the cen-
trality of the kingdom of God in the ministry of Christ that he never
defined it. What seems likely then is that the meaning of the kingdom of God was commonly understood by Jesus' contemporaries or
that it was defined in his own words and deeds. As we shall see, both
appear to be true, at least in part.

Whatever Jesus' contemporaries understood the kingdom of God
to be, they did not find in Jesus the king they had hoped for and
expected. While Jesus interpreted his life and ministry in terms of
inaugurating the kingdom, his idea of kingship differed from that

of his contemporaries.

When John the Baptist announced the coming of the kingdom, he saw it as the time of the great judgment and the establishing of God's righteous rule (Mt 3:7-12). Whatever he anticipated, he soon had doubts whether Jesus was fulfilling them. "When John heard in prison what Christ was doing, he sent his disciples to ask him, 'Are you the one who was to come, or should we expect someone else?' " (Mt 11:2-3).

The Jews of the first century, including Jesus' disciples, anticipated the coming of a kingdom which would be ethnic and geographical. In Mark 10:35-37, James and John ask Jesus for cabinet appointments in his coming kingdom. The crowds which followed Jesus were thinking along the same lines. "Blessed is he who comes in the name of the Lord! Blessed is the coming kingdom of our father David!" (Mk 11:9-10). "The people thought that the kingdom of God was going to appear at once" (Lk 19:11). They wanted the restoration of the Davidic dynasty, and when it became clear that Jesus was not the Messiah they had anticipated, their "Hosannahs" readily turned to "Crucify him, crucify him."

As we begin to see the kingdom of God as defined by what Jesus said and did, we discover that Jesus' enemies and friends did not expect too much of the kingdom, but too little. Jesus came not simply to bring political liberation to one nation, but to bring spiritual, physical and relational liberation to all people. He came not merely to dethrone Caesar, but to destroy the evil force behind all unsanctioned power, Satan himself. He came to bring not just privilege for the few but forgiveness of sin and right standing with God for all.

This comprehensive salvation which Jesus brought into the world was foreshadowed in Genesis 3:15. When man and woman were judged for rebelling against God, the one who tempted them to rebel was judged also. The tempter's judgment was that one day, a man born of woman would rise up and crush his head. The Gospels present Jesus as the fulfillment of that judgment. John tells us, "The reason the Son of God appeared was to destroy the devil's work" (1 Jn 3:8). Jesus Christ came as the last Adam to heal the damage caused by the first Adam (Rom 5:15-19). His reconciling and restoring work will result one day in the healing of all creation (Rom 8:19-21).

The kingdom which Jesus brings to the world is not political, but it is nevertheless concrete and worldly. The kingdom of God addresses not only our internal spiritual state but also our outward physical and social environment. The physical miracles of Christ are not merely symbols of his kingly authority but part of the essence of his kingdom and the means of its advancement. His acts of healing and deliverance were and are weapons of assault against Satan's pseudokingdom.

When Christ began his public ministry, he immediately engaged the enemy in battle and won victories over him. Jesus' conquest over Satan was evidenced in the casting out of demons, healing the sick and raising the dead. Satan continually lost ground against the advance of Christ's kingdom rule because Jesus had bound the strong man and was now plundering his house (Mt 12:29).

Driving Out Demons

In discussing the coming of the kingdom of God in the ministry of Jesus, George E. Ladd states:

> Our Lord's ministry and announcement of the Good News of the kingdom were characterized by healing, and most notably by casting out of demons. He proclaimed the Good News of the kingdom of God, and he demonstrated the Good News of the kingdom of God by delivering men from the bondage of Satan.[1]

In Matthew 12:28, Jesus proclaimed, "If I drive out demons by the Spirit of God, then the kingdom of God has come upon you." The demons themselves were well aware of the significance of what was occurring when Jesus drove them out. On the occasion of Jesus' first public sermon, a man in the synagogue who was possessed by an evil spirit cried out, "What do you want with us, Jesus of Nazareth? Have you come to destroy us?" (Mk 1:24). The answer to this question is yes! Anglican priest, Kenneth Leech emphatically states:

> The coming of the kingdom and the achievement of spiritual freedom is seen in terms of the setting free of individuals and of creation from slavery to these powers. Christ has conquered the powers. This is not a peripheral belief in the New Testament but rather an altogether central article of faith. Jesus' exorcisms stood at the heart of his work.[2]

There was confusion among Jesus' contemporaries regarding the character and scope of demonic powers in the world. They believed that evil powers were chaotic, uncoordinated and undisciplined, "a kingdom divided." In Mark 3:22-27, the scribes from Jerusalem said that Jesus' power to cast out demons was itself demonic; that is, by the power of a greater demon, lesser demons were cast out. Jesus condemned them for attributing to Satan the work of the Holy Spirit and explained that if one demon cast out another, then the evil kingdom is divided and it cannot stand. Jesus implied that evil is not a divided kingdom or even a loose federation, but rather a disciplined force, now waging a defensive war against the offensive advance of the kingdom of God.

The advance of the kingdom of God is successful because Satan, the "strong man," is bound by Jesus, the "stronger" man (Lk 11:21-22). Satan's "house" is this age, and the strong man's "possessions" being "carried off" are men and women previously bound by Satan. The coming of Christ was in some way the binding of Satan or the breaking of his power. Prior to the advent of Jesus, Satan was the god of this world; now his power is more than disputed; it is bound, that is, it now has boundaries. And those boundaries are tightened with every victory of the kingdom of God.

I once viewed a map of Saudi Arabia that helped me conceptualize the advance of the kingdom of God and the retreat of the pseudokingdom of Satan. The line on the map which indicated the external border of Saudi Arabia was solid. The lines which defined the various internal borders (the equivalent of state and provincial border lines) were broken or dotted. I was told that these broken or dotted lines showed the boundaries between the various subkingdoms within the country. These internal boundary lines were not solid because the boundaries shifted, depending upon the relative strength of the various subkingdoms at any given time. When a particular sheik or local ruler ascended in wealth and power, he was able to control more land and so his borders expanded, while his neighbor's decreased.

As Jesus advanced the kingdom of God, the boundaries of Satan's pseudokingdom shrank. The assault of the kingdom was carried on not just by Jesus personally, but also by his followers. Just as Jesus was sent to preach the kingdom and heal the sick, so he sent others to do the same. The followers of Jesus discovered as they went that even demons submitted to them in his name (Lk 10:17). As Jesus listened to this report, he exclaimed that he had seen Satan fall (v. 18). The foundations of Satan's pseudokingdom were breaking up, his rule was successfully challenged and defeated. The kingdom of God was at long last brought to bear on a world of darkness.

The pseudokingdom of Satan is very much like the ancient walled city of Jericho. As Joshua, armed with the authority of God, advanced against Jericho, the city trembled, shook and ultimately fell to its destruction. Every time I minister to demonized people, I sense what Joshua must have felt—that the enemy in them is cornered and terrified and that it's only a matter of time till it is driven from the land. Many Christians have an unfounded fear of the demonic. It is true that we should not take the demonic lightly, but we must never forget that all demonic power has been once and for all bound by the Lord Jesus Christ. Followers of this same Jesus are now to continue looting the "strong man's" house by confidently leading his former captives out into freedom.

Healing the Sick

The creation's deliverance from the power of Satan by the assault of the kingdom of God also means the healing of the sick. As Herman Ridderbos explains,

> The factual relation between the coming of the kingdom and Jesus' miracles is brought out not only by the casting out of devils but also by Jesus' other miracles, for they all prove that Satan's power has been broken and that, therefore, the kingdom has come. At the same time it appears that disease is considered to be generally a consequence of Satan's rule and that Jesus' struggle against the Evil one is not fought solely in the field of ethics but in the whole of the physical domain.[3]

The concrete reality of the coming of the kingdom was evidenced in the defeat and driving off of sickness. It is all but impossible for modern Western people to see sickness the way Jesus understood it. For him, sickness was not explained in terms of germs or biological malfunctions but in terms of personalized evil.

Jesus saw Satan as the cause of all kinds of physical suffering. "On a Sabbath Jesus was teaching in one of the synagogues, and a woman was there who had been crippled by a spirit for eighteen years. She was bent over and could not straighten up at all" (Lk 13:10-11). A modern X-ray would probably have revealed a spinal curvature, and we would tend to look no further. Jesus' diagnosis, however, included the spiritual cause. Jesus did not verbally address the demon in her in order to drive it out; he simply said, "Woman, you are set free from your infirmity" (v. 12).

This raises the question of how often, when the text states that Jesus healed the sick, it included the driving off of a spirit. Not all of the physical sicknesses Jesus healed were linked to demons, but as Werner Foerster notes,

> nevertheless, it may be said that the existence of sickness in this world belongs to the character of [this age] of which Satan is prince. . . . Thus, while not all sicknesses are the work of demons,

they may all be seen as the work of Satan.[4]

In this connection we note Jesus' use of the word *rebuke* in physical healings. Jesus *rebuked* demons (Mk 9:25) and also *rebuked* Peter's mother-in-law's fever (Lk 4:39). Modern medicine would likely have attributed the fever to an infection. Jesus apparently regarded the fever, or the power behind it, as personalized evil. Other diseases in the Gospel story which today might be analyzed as deafness (Mt 12:22), as epilepsy (Mk 9:14-19) or as arthritis (Lk 13:10-17) are linked by Jesus to Satan. Where we see germs behind sickness, Jesus saw Satan's whip. Kenneth Leech concurs:

> The coming of God's kingdom and the achievement of spiritual freedom is seen in terms of the setting free of individuals and of creation from slavery to these powers. . . . The cases in the Synoptic Gospels were cases of disease for which we would today offer a different kind of explanation—mental disturbances, epilepsy, convulsions, dumbness, blindness. . . . What is crucial is that in all the cases, physical and mental healing was accompanied by the setting free of a person from oppression, from those forces which stunted and distorted his humanity.[5]

Occasionally while praying for the sick, we uncover the presence of an unclean spirit which is somehow, directly or indirectly, connected to the physical symptoms of illness. These are often confronted directly and expelled, resulting in a healing. Some time ago, we prayed over a woman who suffered constant migraine headaches since her college days. We prayed repeatedly regarding the physical symptoms with no effect. Finally, one member of our team said she thought a spirit was causing the pain. She then rebuked the spirit, and the pain, which had remained constant throughout the session, lifted immediately. It has now been eighteen months since this event, and the woman has remained free of migraine pain.

A young man, who recently converted to Christ out of the occult, came to me for help when his hands became spastic. As he walked through my living room door, he held out his hands which resembled bird's claws. He was being medically tested for neurological disease, but he wanted prayer as well. I began to pray for him and almost immediately sensed a spirit. I confronted it; it showed itself and then left. Within a few minutes, the young man's hands were back to normal and have remained so.

A while back I received a report from a medical college in Pennsylvania entitled "Prayer-Meeting Cardioversion." It told the story of an eighty-three-year-old Black Baptist woman who was being treated for atrial fibrillation (rapid irregular heartbeat) who was "healed" when her pastor and daughters commanded "this evil rhythm to leave her body." In that instant, "The patient reported feeling as though cats and dogs were running out of my chest." A nurse with a direct view of a cardiac monitor reported that "at that moment, sinus rhythm was restored. Atrial fibrillation did not recur."[6]

The medical people who observed and reported this event would not likely see the kingdom of God at work in it. The reason is that our view of sickness is different from that of Jesus and his contemporaries. We now have microscopes and a different anthropology. Today we distinguish between body and soul, the ancient Hebrews did not. Jesus and his hearers correlated salvation with the physical as well as the spiritual. Saving the whole person constituted deliverance from the dominion of sin and Satan.

Michael Green notes that

we suffer today from a false distinction between the secular and the sacred, the physical and the spiritual. The Christian church has sometimes behaved as though only the spiritual element in man was the subject of God's concern. The actions of Jesus as recorded in the Gospels give the lie to this, and show that God's salvation concerns the whole man (Mark 3:4). Indeed the word [salvation] is used most frequently in the Gospels with reference to the healing of disease.[7]

In Scripture, the forgiveness of sin, eternal life, deliverance from spiritual bondage and healing are bound up into one comprehensive salvation.

In Mark 5:23, 5:34, 6:56 and 10:52, the words "to heal" or "make whole" are translated from the Greek word *sozo*, which also means "to save." Even when a sickness was clearly the consequence of sin, Jesus treated it as belonging to the larger disease of evil. Jesus' power over sickness was the same as his power over sin. This is the logic in the story of the paralyzed man, lowered to Jesus through the roof in Mark 2:1-12. Jesus' authority to save from sickness is the same as his authority to save from sin.

We often witness this same power of Jesus' comprehensive salvation when praying for people with sin-caused illness. In sexually transmitted disease, the connection between sin and sickness seems clear. Time and again we have heard the confession of sexual sin, pronounced Christ's forgiveness and in his name healed the sickness. In doing so, we participate in the whole salvation Jesus brought. As the kingdom of God advances in this way, the dominion of Satan is driven back. Only in the last day, when we receive our resurrected bodies, will salvation be complete.

Raising the Dead

The ultimate expression of the kingdom's victory over evil occurred as Jesus returned life to those who had died. Catholic theologian Raymond Brown observes:

> Death as a by-product of man's sin was a particularly strong element in Satan's dominion. As Paul puts it, "The last enemy to be destroyed is death" (I Corinthians 15:26). Thus in raising from the dead Jesus manifests an especially strong interven tion . . . and reveals that God has visited his people.[8]

The most awful weapon of Satan's realm is death. If Jesus intended to comfort and defeat the "strong man," he had to meet this adversary in the valley of the shadow of death where he was strongest. Here Jesus met and defeated the enemy in two stages. First, in the course of his own ministry, Jesus gave life back to those who had lost it. This, however, was like all other physical healings, only partial and provisional. Those raised from the dead would die again.

The definitive defeat of Satan occurred in Jesus' death and resurrection. This reality was the key note of the apostles' teaching. In Colossians 2:15, Paul states that Jesus disarmed the evil powers and "made a public spectacle of them, triumphing over them by the cross." When John announced that "the reason the Son of God appeared was to destroy the devil's work" (1 Jn 3:8), he stated it in the past tense. This is not a prophecy about Christ's second coming—it is a statement about his first coming. Christ is King, Satan is a defeated enemy, and this is most evident in Jesus' victory over death and God's promise of our own resurrection at Christ's return.

This is why we can say with Paul that, though we face death, it has lost its victory and its sting (1 Cor 15:55). And we can also anticipate the possibility of raising people from the dead as a part of our pastoral ministry.

Jesus' contemporaries misunderstood the kingdom of God. They hoped it was the recapitulation of a past glory. We may misunderstand it by seeing it only as some spiritual state or future event. The kingdom of God came through Jesus as a concrete reality which reaches one person at a time. As each person was in some way delivered by Christ from the dominion of darkness, the kingdom advanced. It continues to advance in the same way today—one deliverance, one healing, one conversion at a time. This view not only helps us to understand the kingdom of God, it also accounts for the uneven quality and quantity of healing today, which we will consider next.

CHAPTER SEVEN

THE FIGHT IS REAL

THE EBB AND FLOW IN THE COSMIC BATTLE BETWEEN LIGHT and darkness is not a dance choreographed by a puppeteer Deity. The fight is real. The victory of Christ through his cross and resurrection is final, but not yet fully realized. Evil continues to exercise its bounded, though significant, power till Christ returns in his glory.

The presence of the kingdom, as manifest in healing, is now only partial because we live between the time of Christ's coming and his coming again. As Thomas Smail notes,

> In the realm of healing much happens to authenticate Christ's present will and power to heal the otherwise incurable, and yet, often distressingly enough fails to happen to serve to remind us that we are not yet in the last day, and to leave the mystery of the

"not-yet" all around us.[1]

The "mystery of the 'not-yet' all around us," includes the reality of Satan's actual freedom and power. Many Christians are uncomfortable with the idea that Satan could in any significant way oppose God, that there could be a real struggle between them. There is, however, real evil in the world, operating without divine sanction. This is because the good and sovereign God has willed that angels and human beings be free to choose and therefore also be free to choose evil.

As Dorothy Sayers observes, these real choices are followed by real consequences:

> All things God can do, but this thing He will not: Unbind the chain of cause and consequence, or speed time's arrow backward. When man chose to know like God, he also chose to be judged by God's values.[2]

God's fight with evil is real because it is an inherent impossibility for him to give freedom and not allow that freedom to be used.

The Possible and the Impossible

Some things are impossible for us to do but not impossible for God—like parting the Red Sea and resurrecting the dead. Other things are not just impossible for us, but they are also intrinsically or inherently impossible. Making a tree all red and green at exactly the same time, for instance, is not just hard to do; it is impossible. It is nonsense. Giving freedom and denying the possibility of evil is this kind of impossibility. Sir John Eccles and Daniel Robinson put it this way:

> How, it is asked, can an all-powerful and all-benevolent God permit man to commit palpable unjust acts against innocent persons? And the answer, which is so obvious as to seem erroneous, is that it is impossible, it is logically impossible to attach responsibility for actions over which the actor has absolutely no control. To the extent that we are morally responsible for what we do we

must be free to do it. Even God cannot violate the law of contradiction.[3]

In a concrete moral world not even God can prevent his creatures
from making evil choices which inevitably result in suffering. Nonsense is not transformed to sense simply by prefixing the nonsense
with "God can." To say that God could, if he chose to, prevent all
suffering in our kind of world is nonsense. The kind of world in
which God will eventually eliminate all suffering is not the one we
live in now, but the "new heaven and the new earth" to come. A
world where God's will is done means the end of life as we presently
know it.

The Fight against Evil

In the meantime, as we live life between the first and second com-
ings of Christ, God achieves his plan not by divine fiat but by
fighting for it. The victory of God through Christ was not decreed
but was won by the shedding of human tears and the spilling of real
blood. Refusing to wield his infinite power, God won the battle with
evil through the apparent weakness of sacrificial love. He did not
cast his enemies out from the heights but drove them out from the
depths.

Or as Colin Brown puts it:

In the last analysis, as the cross itself demonstrates, the ultimate
victory is won through the self-surrender of Christ in weakness
and not through a display of force. Paradoxically, the way of
weakness is the way of strength. . . . Miracles give glimpses of the
glory to come. But the way to glory is the way of the cross.[4]

God's power is not impersonal force, but it is power with character.
The controlling center of that character is love which was expressed
through the humanity of Christ and is now revealed through his
church.

Satan was defeated not by raw power but through Christ's loving
obedience to the Father. The beginning of the end of Satan's grip

on the world occurred during the temptation of Jesus (Mt 4:1-11). Satan sought to subvert the Son of God by offering him all the kingdoms of the world (v. 8). Satan would give them up without a struggle but for a price (v. 9). Jesus resisted this temptation, and the battle for the dominion of God's creation was joined.

Throughout Jesus' ministry, this battle was characterized by an ebb and flow. There were victories and losses on both sides. By the "finger of God" Jesus drove out demons (Lk 11:20) at one point. And at another, Jesus confessed that this is the "hour when darkness reigns" (Lk 22:53). Finally, with Jesus on the cross, it appeared that Satan had won. But on the third day the deathblow to Satan's pseudo-kingdom was dealt.

It is not just in the broad story line that there is an ebb and flow in the battle, but also in the specific circumstances of everyday life. In Matthew 12:43-45, Jesus explains that even if the kingdom should at first drive evil out of a person, that evil may return seven times stronger, if not prevented. The evil spirit may return to its prey because the enemy is not as yet banished from the earth. Jesus makes it clear that the opposition has not been removed from the battle-field, merely driven back.

Again, when Jesus delivers the demon-possessed man in Luke 8:26-33, the demons at first resist and withstand the command of Jesus to come out (vv. 28-29). Jesus does not simply decree that demons be gone; he fights them. The demons, having seen that they were beaten by the "stronger man," begged him not to throw them into the abyss, but rather to send them into a nearby herd of pigs (vv. 31-33). On the one hand, they knew that they were subject to Jesus' authority; and, on the other hand, they believed that it was not yet their time to be consigned to the abyss.

When Jesus gave them permission to go into the pigs, it was for their provisional self-survival. He allowed them to stay on the field of battle for a season. We are no doubt encountering these same demons today. Jesus did not put an end to Satan's power, rather he bound it so that we may have authority over it.

The Ultimate Victory

A careful exegesis of this and other relevant passages teaches us about Satan's significant power and his real opposition to the will of God. At the same time, such a study prevents us from straying into a cosmological dualism—that is, a view of the cosmos which sees the forces of good and evil, light and darkness, God and Satan, as being of equal power in their struggle against each other. While it is true that Satan has significant power and constitutes real opposition, he is a creature and through the Creator God-Man, Jesus Christ, he has been bound. In viewing the battle between Jesus and Satan, G. C. Berkouwer states:

> Once again, it is necessary to observe that this battle is not a contest of mere force against force. Rather, the power of Satan is "broken down" by the power of him in whom salvation and power are bound together in perfect unity. The unity of battle and sacrifice, victory and atonement.[5]

Or we could say that through his authentic life, perfect sacrifice and victorious resurrection Jesus effected a transfer of sovereignty from the pseudokingdom to the real kingdom. Now Jesus is seen to possess all authority in heaven and earth (Mt 28:18). God always had this authority, but through the Incarnation it is established in history. And the implications of Jesus' "all authority" are now manifest through the church in history.

Satan is bound and his pseudokingdom is breaking up, yet God has left him room to maneuver. What power and freedom he still possesses and precisely when he is able to exercise these is not entirely clear from Scripture. What is clear from Scripture and increasingly confirmed in our experience is that the kingdom of God has already absorbed the full wrath of Satan's might and survived it. The kingdom of God has already gone through its darkest night. The most dismal evil in all history found its absolute limits at Calvary. After evil had choked on its own venom, it became forever subject to Christ and to us in his name. There is no absolute dualism between God and Satan. The victor at the end of the battle is already crowned. Yet there are still many sick and some demonized people among us who are subjected to the unsanctioned and illegal power of Satan. How are we to understand this ambiguity?

A helpful illustration of how a war already won could continue to be fought comes from the history of World War 2. On "D-Day" the allied troops landed successfully at Normandy beach in order to establish a secure beachhead on the European mainland. It was understood by military experts at the time that this operation secured ultimate victory for the allies. There would be, however, many more bloody battles fought before "V-E Day," the day on which ultimate victory would be realized.

In God's war with evil, "D-Day" occurred with the death and resurrection of Christ. Ultimate victory is now assured; yet the fight rages on till "V-E Day," the glorious return of Christ. Between these times, the church presses the battle against the evil which remains in the world. Blood is still shed in these battles, and some of the blood will be ours, but we are assured that the ultimate victory of the past will be fully realized in the future.

Figure 1 displays visually the relationships between the present evil age, the promise of redemption and the age to come. Notice the "now and not yet" which characterizes the period between the "D-Day" of the cross and the "V-E Day" of Christ's return.

Being preoccupied with the problem of pain as an intellectual exercise would be to miss our calling as the church of Jesus Christ. We have not been given intellectual answers to the problem of evil; rather, we are given authority and power over it. God has sovereignly brought about "D-Day." And he will sovereignly bring about "V-E Day." Between these times, the effectiveness of the kingdom of God against evil is in part contingent on the obedience of the church. Our faithfulness in the fight is the issue we consider next.

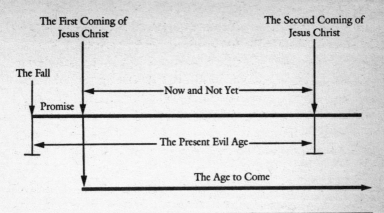

Figure 1.

CHAPTER EIGHT

OUR FAITH IN THE FIGHT

PASTOR GAYLE ERWIN PUTS PERSPECTIVE ON THE RELATION between faith and healing when he says:

One of my running arguments with God is that not enough people are healed to please me. His running argument with me is that I both fail to pray for them and fail to walk with them through their recovery. Healing is something I don't understand. I have seen enough to believe that it occurs and is not always psychologically explainable. But I have also seen enough to know that the pop theologies which clobber the sheep for not having enough faith are inadequate. When Jesus walked on the earth, He healed the sick freely. In some places He healed all the sick . . . only occasionally did Jesus compliment outstanding faith, yet He continued to heal. The only place He didn't do much healing was where disbelief was the major attitude.[1]

Those who have read the New Testament realize the vital importance of faith in relating to God. To be related to him at all implies faith. Beyond this, we receive gifts from him and do work for him through faith (Gal 3:5). Mind-boggling things can be done in faith (Mk 11:22-24). Whatever faith is, we do not need much of it to work wonders. If we only have a tiny speck of it, "nothing will be impossible" for us (Mt 17:20-21). On the other hand, even something relatively simple like driving out a demon cannot be done without at least this tiny speck (Mt 17:20).

The Link between Faith and Healing

In my criticism of "faith formula" in part one, I stated that there is no strict cause-and-effect relationship between faith and healing. Nevertheless, the exercise of faith is regarded as significant and even determinative in the Gospel healing stories.

For that matter, most references to faith in the Gospels occur in relationship to Jesus' healings. Christ looked for faith (Mt 9:28; Mk 9:23). He congratulated people when they demonstrated it (Mt 8:10; 9:22; 15:28). And he rebuked people when they failed to exercise it (Lk 9:41). Jesus was constantly on the lookout for faith and appeared eager to reward it. Obviously, then, we should cultivate faith and learn to exercise it, especially in the ministry of healing.

When confronted by the New Testament teaching on faith's relationship to healing, we see that there is a vital link between the two. But the precise nature of that link is difficult to understand for two reasons: (1) sometimes the biblical teaching on faith and healing is complicated, and (2) at other times biblical teaching seems unrealistic to the modern mind.

These intellectual difficulties are intensified when we add to them personal experiences in praying for the sick. Many of us have been confused and hurt when those we prayed for were not healed. My best friend died of a brain hemorrhage three years ago, and my secretary died of cancer a month ago. I prayed in "faith" for both. One of my goddaughters remains deaf despite my faithful intercession for her.

The "not-yet" of the coming of the kingdom of God is all around us. It seems that our faith sometimes contributes to a healing and at other times appears to have little effect. These ambiguities keep us from making dogmatic pronouncements on faith's relationship to healing, but they do not explain or excuse the characteristic shyness among evangelicals in praying for the sick. I believe that the caution and even pessimism displayed by most of us in this matter is not due primarily to "honest intellectual questions" or even hurtful experiences, but primarily to a generalized mood of despair. Broadly speaking, evangelical Christians respond to many of life's ills fatalistically—retreating from them rather than combating them.

Until recently, most evangelical Christians subscribed to a "lifeboat" theology that sees the world sliding into the apostasy and judgment of the end times. Many believers thought the best we could hope for was to get ourselves and a few converts into the lifeboat of "eternal salvation" before history sank in the flames of the final holocaust. Trying to do something about problems in the world was generally regarded as futile—at best it was polishing the brass on a sinking ship. This is why, until recently, we have been all but silent on social and political issues.

Evangelical Christians claim to believe the Bible, and we do regarding the historical events it records. We have faith in what Jesus did two thousand years ago, but we are often crippled with doubt when asked to believe what he might do today. No matter what eschatological beliefs we hold, we all affirm unflinchingly that Jesus will exercise great power in the end times, purging the world of every vestige of evil. We have faith that God did great things in the past and will again do great things, but we often doubt that he will do great things today. This kind of evangelical "faith" relegates God and us to perpetual inactivity. It is not difficult, therefore, to see why many of us are timid in praying for the sick.

What Faith Is Not
Before I explain the kind of faith I think Jesus is looking for today in our healing ministries, I want to say one more word about what faith is not. In reacting against pessimism and passivity, some people may adopt a simplistic triumphalism—that is to say, they may look at faith as hard work and strong belief by which we may ensure God's blessing.

But faith is not a work by which God's favor is earned or his hand moved. We cannot bring in the kingdom or even produce an evidence of the kingdom through our own efforts. Old Testament and intertestamental Jewish history make this abundantly clear. According to John Bright and George Ladd, the members of the Israelite community who perpetuated the hope of the kingdom of God believed that if only they kept the Law, the kingdom would come.[2]

Following their return from exile in Babylon, Israel was, in fact, purged of explicit idolatry, which many of them assumed had till then prevented God's kingdom from coming. It was popularly maintained in Israel that the kingdom would come now that Israel was free from idolatry and was keeping the Law. This chronic tendency among religious people to think that our goodness causes God's blessing was painfully disabused. Ladd explains that following the great exile,

> Israel was no longer an apostate, backsliding people; she was devoted to her God and obedient to his law. She spurned idolatry and meticulously separated herself from uncleanness. . . . Still the kingdom did not come. History was shot through with evils for which there was no prophetic explanation.[3]

Their disappointment and frustration gradually gave way to pessimism.

> The blessings of the kingdom cannot be experienced in the present, for this age is abandoned to evil and suffering. Such a

theology was forced upon devout Jews as the only possible explanation for their evil plight. Israel was obedient to the Law but yet did not find deliverance. The solution to the problem of evil was thrown altogether into the future.[4]

They concluded from their experience that it was the lot of the righteous to suffer in the present evil age (our modern equivalent is "getting stepped on for Jesus"). Only a sovereign act of God, that is, the inbreaking of the kingdom of God, could secure their salvation now.

When the kingdom of God did come in Jesus Christ, it came with power to save and deliver from evil. But it came partially and provisionally. The expected salvation of all Israel and the anticipated recreation of the cosmos did not happen. Not all Israel saw the kingdom of God come. Not all experienced its salvation. Not all the sick and demonized were healed. The kingdom of God was offered initially to only a few of his children in Israel.

In order for these select few to experience kingdom salvation in reconciliation, healing and deliverance, they had to receive it in faith. The evidence of the kingdom of God in healing, for instance, was not an act of sheer power. It was an expression of love offered freely and received in faith within the larger context of God's covenant relationship with Israel. This is why Jesus told his disciples not to go to the Gentiles with the message of the kingdom (Mt 10:5). A covenant relationship with them had not yet been established. It was to the "lost sheep of Israel" that the message of the kingdom must first go. It was to them that healing and deliverance was initially offered (Mt 10:6-8). In the first coming of Jesus, the kingdom of God was not universally imposed as it will be one day. Instead, it was personally received or rejected.

In Mark 6:5-6 we read of Jesus that when he visited his hometown, "He could not do any miracles there. . . . And he was amazed at their lack of faith." The signs of the kingdom are manifested among those in relationship to God in response to their faith. God is free to offer his love, but he does not compel others to receive it. When we assert God's freedom, we do not mean that he forces his love on others.

Forced love is an inherent impossibility. As Ladd explains,

This is the mystery of the kingdom: that the kingdom of God has come among men and yet men can reject it. The kingdom will not experience uniform success. Not all will receive it. . . . One day God will indeed manifest His mighty power to purge the earth of wickedness, sin and evil; but not now. God's kingdom is working among men, but God will not compel them to bow before it. They must receive it; the response must come from a willing heart and a submissive will. God is still dealing with us in this same way.[5]

When Jesus was prevented from doing miracles in his hometown, it was not because he needed the moral support of the crowd or that he made legalistic demands. His miracles required a context—they could only be performed in the context of personal relationships, relationships of trust and receptivity. Jesus could not impose that relationship. It had to be entered into freely. The question is not whether Jesus had power to work miracles in all circumstances, but whether he was free to exercise his power in all circumstances.

This is why Jesus refuses to attempt a miracle when one is demanded of him. When Satan insists on a sign from Jesus to validate his status as Son of God, Jesus refuses (Mt 4:3-4). There is obviously no context for a miracle. Again, in Matthew 12:38-39, the Pharisees ask Jesus for a sign as infallible proof that Jesus is who he claims to be. But Jesus' miracles are not primarily apologetic in nature. In themselves they prove nothing anyway. His healing acts are expressions of divine mercy to be received in faith. Faith to be healed means being open to God's love. Faith to pray for the sick means openness to being a vessel of that love. As Thomas Smail says,

Power outside the context of love and truth is precisely that to which the enemy tempted Jesus in the wilderness, and to which for example the church in Corinth is tempted again so that it has to be reminded that charismata exercised outside the context of love and truth are worth nothing at all (1 Corinthians 13).[6]

The Faith to Be Healed

The faith to be healed and to pray for the sick is nothing other than childlike trust in the loving character and purpose of our Heavenly Father. My wife and I have discovered that people who find it hard to trust God are often difficult to pray for. If they cannot be vulnerable before him, they are unlikely to be healed. The primary need in these cases is not to heap condemnation on them for not believing, but rather to seek first their spiritual healing. As people are healed in their relationship to God and become more open to him, other healings are more likely.

This relational orientation to an understanding of faith should keep us from the errors of some popular faith teachers who define faith as psychological certainty. In shifting our focus from the character of God to our private state of mind, their approach weakens, rather than strengthens, faith. When we are exhorted, for instance, to expel all vestiges of doubt from our mind before we can be healed, we are damaged psychologically and misled theologically. True Christian faith in all its expressions looks away from self to God and what he has done for us in Jesus Christ. The real question is not, "Do I believe strongly enough to be healed or to pray for the sick?" but, "Is God the sort of person I can trust, and am I willing to be open to his love?"

As we look away from our own state of mind to God's grace revealed in Jesus Christ, we see that just as Israel was related to God through the covenant of Sinai so we are related to God through the new covenant in Christ's blood. As the kingdom was made known to Israel through Jesus of Nazareth, so it is now made known to the church by the pouring out of God's Holy Spirit. Saturating our minds with the truth of God's unconditional love will do more to create a healing environment than anything else we may do.

Faith to be healed and to pray for healing can come to us just as it did to those who gathered around Jesus. As we look at Jesus in the New Testament and believe what we see, we find the freedom to trust him. We see in him the character of the person we can trust with our entire beings. There is never any thought that we can demand healing or claim it from him, but there is freedom to trust him for it because it is so obviously the very thing he wants to do.

Being assured of our complete acceptance by God through Christ and knowing his will in Christ will enable us not only to pray for healing but also to persevere if necessary. Our experience is that most healings are not instantaneous but progressive. Persistent prayer is invaluable in this process.

Faith, rooted not in faith but in the God of the New Testament, does not disappoint. Regardless of the outcome of prayers for healing, our faith in Jesus Christ need not falter. We will continue to live under the shadow of the "not-yet." Though we are once healed, we may become sick again, and we will in the end die. But in and through it all we see Jesus Christ, the faithful God.

And when we think of Satan and his work against us, we see him as Jesus did, hurled down from the place which he falsely usurped. When we think of demons, we see them as defeated foes escaping into the pigs only to be destroyed in the sea. When we think of the grave, we remember that it had to release Lazarus at Christ's command. When we look at the cross, we see the very worst evil that could ever happen. And in the resurrection we see that evil judged and its effects healed.

Faith to heal the sick is not bravado—it is the freedom to believe and act based on who Jesus Christ is. Our faith in the fight to heal is expressed in our acting, despite our doubts, on who we see Jesus to be.

In our experience, there is a high correlation between our *asking* God for healing and healing coming about. We know that God does not have to heal, but he does heal. We have also observed that there are variables and contingencies which enter into the healing event, often opposing it. We now consider the inevitable ambiguity created by these variables and contingencies.

CHAPTER NINE

THE VICTORY PRESENT
AND FUTURE

IN OUR KIND OF WORLD, THE AUTHORITY OF THE KINGDOM OF God is not universally enforced. We see the ebb and flow of God's power even in the life of Jesus Christ. Early in Jesus' ministry, he walked on water. Towards the end, he could not even carry his own cross. The real presence of the kingdom of God is sometimes clothed in apparent weakness.

The New Testament community was confronted with the ambiguity of God's power in the ministry of healing. They seemed to have faced this mystery in a natural, matter-of-fact way. We read that they regularly experienced healing power among them, and we also see Christians in their community who were not healed. Trophimus, for instance, was left sick at Miletus by the great apostle Paul himself (2 Tim 4:20). Epaphroditus was ill and almost died (Phil 2:26-27).

Timothy had a persistent stomach disorder for which Paul prescribed some medicinal wine. On another occasion, however, when Paul was stranded on Malta, he prayed and all the sick were healed (Acts 28:9).

Victory Now But Not Complete

The ministry of healing, like all other aspects of Christian ministry and experience, is partial, provisional and ambiguous. Preachers reading this, for instance, will recall some Sunday mornings when their preaching has been inspired and powerfully effective and other Sunday mornings when it has not been. Evangelists constantly struggle with the ambiguous character of the coming of the kingdom of God. Not everyone responds to God through their messages; yet God wills that all should be saved and has made provision for them (2 Pet 3:9).

We see the now-and-not-yet nature of the kingdom not just through our ministries but also in our personal experience of salvation. We have already been remade in God's image (Eph 1:13), we are progressively being remade in his image (2 Cor 3:18), and one day in the future we will be perfectly remade in his image (Phil 3:20-21). Or, to put it another way, we were saved (2 Tim 1:9), we are in the process of being saved (Phil 2:12-13), and at some future time we will be saved (1 Pet 1:9). When the child of God is asked "Are you saved?" the proper answer is yes and no, now-and-not-yet. We have entered the kingdom of God (Jn 3:3), we must enter it through many hardships (Acts 14:22), and we will one day enter it (Rev 5:10).

Freedom from sin and sickness is eschatological—that is, it comes finally and fully only with the eschaton, the end of time that comes with the return of Jesus Christ. Full freedom will come only with our resurrection. Yet freedom has already come, and we experience it now in partial yet real ways through following Jesus Christ. As John Bright explains,

[Jesus'] miracles are "mighty works" . . . of the kingdom of God, which in them advertises its presence; they are a taste of "the powers of the age to come" (Hebrews 6:5). In them the grip of the Adversary—who has enthralled men in bonds of disease, madness, death, and sin—begins to be loosened. . . . The kingdom of God, then, is a power already released in the world. True, its beginnings are tiny, and it might seem incredible that the humble ministry of this obscure Galilean could be the dawning of a new age of God. Yet it is! What has begun here will surely go on to its conclusion; nothing can stop it. And the conclusion is victory.[1]

Christ's victory over the evil forces in life was not for the early church a mere doctrine but a reality. They did not arrive at the conviction that Jesus was victor in theory, but through the experience of obedience. The early Christians were those who had actually "tasted the goodness of the word of God and the powers of the coming age" (Heb 6:5).

Prior to the coming of the Lord Jesus Christ, they had little defense against Satanic bondage. They were helpless before "the ruler of the kingdom of the air" (Eph 2:2) and subject to the evil one who had the whole world under his control (1 Jn 5:19). Now, however, they discovered in their daily experience that this was no longer true. Something in the essential make-up of the cosmos had changed. Their authority over Satan and his works was not theoretical; it was actual. It was not just an article of faith; it was their experience. It did not have to be hoped for in the future; it could be had now. Everywhere the church went, it proclaimed the resurrection of Christ and that proclamation was effective. As Ladd puts it:

Jesus did not promise the forgiveness of sins; he bestowed it. He did not simply assure men of the future fellowship of the kingdom; he invited men into fellowship with himself as the bearer of the kingdom. He did not merely promise them vindication in the day of judgment; he bestowed upon them a present righteous-

ness. He not only taught an eschatological deliverance from physical evil; he went about demonstrating the redeeming power of
the kingdom, delivering men from sickness and even death.[2]

Parables of the Kingdom

Jesus had carefully taught his followers that the kingdom of God
could be present and real and yet not complete. In Matthew 13 and
Mark 4, Jesus teaches the "parables of the kingdom." In these parables, he offers various ways of understanding the present reality of
the kingdom in tension with its incompleteness.

In Matthew 13:1-23 (the parable of the sower), Jesus explains that
while the kingdom has come, it will for various reasons not experience uniform success. The seed of the kingdom is uniformly good
in itself, but it falls on soil of uneven quality. Some good seed falls
on hard ground and lies there exposed until the evil one snatches
it away. Other good seed falls on rocky, shallow ground. The seed,
eager to grow, sprouts quickly, but since there is no place for it to
set down roots, no environment for sustained growth, the young
plant dies. More good seed falls on thorny places. The seed sprouts,
but the thorns grow up with it and eventually choke it out. Finally,
the good seed falls into deep, clean, receptive soil. It sprouts, grows
and produces a harvest.

The applications here are endless, but Jesus' essential point is that
the success of the kingdom can be snatched away by Satan, it can
be rejected by shallow people, and it can be choked out by the
worries of this life and the deceitfulness of wealth. By this, Jesus
warns us that not all who hear the gospel will receive it, not all
relationships will be reconciled, not all poor people will be fed, not
all the demonized will be delivered, and not all the sick will be
healed.

Sometimes the uneven quality of our healing ministry is starkly
evident. A group of friends and I spent two hours praying over three
people in wheel chairs one evening after a healing seminar. One of

the three was a woman in the final stages of multiple sclerosis, another was a man with a spinal injury which left him paralyzed from the chest down, and the third was an ex-dancer who now could not even stand upright because of severe arthritis.

We prayed with the same love and skill or lack of them for all three, yet at the end of two hours only one was up and walking—the lady with MS. She seemed to have no more faith than the others and claimed to be no more deserving; yet after two years in her chair she got up. Months later and still improving, she is now almost back to normal. The remaining two are grateful for the loving care they received then and since, but are only slightly improved physically.

The parable of the tares (Mt 13:24-30, 36-43) illustrates the same dynamic. In this story, the kingdom of God is like a man who sowed good seed, and an enemy came after him and sowed weeds in the same field. The good seed and the weeds grow up together and remain intertwined until the end of the age when the final separation will occur. Light and darkness, good and evil, health and sickness exist side by side. The kingdom has been sown into the world. The good seed has taken root, but it does not grow uncontested.

The parables of the mustard seed and the yeast (Mt 13:31-35) illustrate another facet of the ambiguous, partial and provisional character of the kingdom of God. Both the mustard seed and yeast seem insignificant. The seed disappears into the ground; the yeast melts into the lump of dough. No one takes notice of its presence at first. But, by its very nature, the mustard seed will one day dominate its world, and the yeast will permeate its environment.

What, might we ask, is the significance of a few healings and deliverances in a world so thoroughly broken and diseased? These parables teach that what seems insignificant today will be fully established tomorrow. Our healings now seem small in light of the enormous need, but these healings are genuine manifestations of the new world coming. The kingdom of God has come among us; we may participate in it now, even in its incompleteness, looking forward to the day of its consummation at the return of Christ.

The Case of Lazarus

Another of the Gospel stories which illustrates the real power of the kingdom alongside its ambiguous, provisional nature is the raising of Lazarus (Jn 11:1-44). This story bristles with paradox. I will mention only a few. First of all, when Jesus heard of Lazarus' terminal illness, "he stayed where he was two more days" (v. 6). In every other instance recorded in the Gospels where Jesus is asked for healing, he gives it freely and promptly. But in this instance Jesus seemingly fails to respond.

Added to the evil of the death is the suffering and pain of mourning (vv. 32-35). Not only did the family of Lazarus weep at his dying, but so did Jesus (v. 35). Here we have the strange scene of Jesus weeping real, not staged, tears over a tragedy which he apparently could have prevented. As some pointed out, the grief of Jesus was suspect. "Could not he who opened the eyes of the blind man have kept this man from dying?" (v. 37). Jesus explains later that all this was so that they might believe (v. 33). That is small comfort, however, to the sisters who from their human vantage point know only that Jesus could have healed their brother but did not.

Then Jesus approaches the grave of his friend and calls him forth by name. Some have suggested that Jesus called Lazarus by name because otherwise he would have emptied the entire cemetery. My question is, So what would be wrong with that? And how many widows and orphans standing there were asking this same question? Lazarus alone comes forth from the grave, but even then only provisionally. In time he will die again and probably be laid in the same grave once more.

This reminds us that no matter how successful our prayers for healing are, they all fail in the end. We all die. Practically speaking, why bring Lazarus back from a death he will experience again? And why heal a person and extend a life which will inevitably suffer death at a later date?

The partiality and provisionality of healing is a smaller part of the larger ambiguity of our entire life in Christ's kingdom. When we are baptized into Christ, we die to sin and come alive to new life in Christ (Rom 6:3). Empirically speaking, however, we are neither totally dead to sin nor completely alive to Christ. And though Christ himself paid the penalty for our sin, we still experience death which results from sin. Only in the resurrection will we experience our final victory over sickness and death.

In this life sin is not totally removed from our experience and neither is sickness. But just as we battle in the power of God to defeat the one, so we also battle in the name of Christ to defeat the other. Just as Christ established boundaries to Satan's power, so he also gives boundaries to the possibilities of our lives. We will not live forever, because death is one of life's boundaries. We may, however, live more free of sickness and sin because evil also has boundaries. The gospel is not just life without boundaries after death, but a full life within new expanded boundaries before death.

Responsible Pastoral Ministry

Assertive Christian ministry, however, needs to guard against pastoral irresponsibility. In making an aggressive attack on sickness by affirming the will and power of God to heal, we may inadvertently do more harm than good to those who are not healed. And in vigorously attending to the demonized and diseased, we may neglect the poor and the hungry who are also objects of Christ's compassion. A balanced agenda and common sense are called for in all ministry.

While it is well and good to be sensitive, we must not draw back. The kingdom has come, and therefore the church should strive to care for all of God's people with appropriate ministry to each. To water down or overqualify the hope of healing in order to protect those who may not be healed only ends in impoverishing everyone involved.

First of all, if we do not hopefully and faithfully pray for the sick, many who could be healed will not be. I know many people now alive, who would not be, and others now well, who would not be, if the church had not prayed for them.

Second, every healing within the Christian community belongs to the entire body, including those who are not healed. The healed one is a sign to all that the resurrection of our bodies, the ultimate act of God's healing ministry, is on the way. Healing is a sacramental event for the entire church. It witnesses to the reality that Christ has come and is coming again. It is a glimpse of the New Heaven and the New Earth.

Third, God normally works on earth incarnationally. God created human beings to exercise dominion on earth under his authority. The fall of the first Adam stripped man and woman of dominion authority. Through the incarnation of the Last Adam that dominion authority is restored. Now, through the followers of the Last Adam, God's authority is expressed, in part, by healing the sick. In drawing back from praying for the sick, we deny God his usual means of working in the world.

Fourth, the basic attitude of restricting hope for fear of disappointment is not realism but pessimism. When we affirm God's will and power to heal, we are not offering false hope to anyone. Our offer is one of reasonable hope. No one approaches anything in Christian ministry with guarantees. There is no certainty that everyone we witness to will believe in Christ, yet we continue to witness. So likewise, while there is no certainty that everyone we pray for will be healed, we continue to pray.

Taking Risks

Risk is inherent in all of life. Faith obviously involves risk. Canon Jim Glennon told me once that he viewed the healing ministry as "walking perpetually on the brink of disaster and on the verge of a miracle." He also told me that in the twenty-five years of his healing ministry in the Anglican Church, "not once has anyone voiced regret after receiving prayer for healing." My much shorter experience confirms this. Not once has anyone complained when we prayed for their healing, even when it did not come. A friend of mine, who recently died of cancer, told me in the last days of her illness, "Even if your prayers don't work, Ken, this experience has been more than worth it. For the first time I have experienced God's love. If I die, I will die alive."

If people are not lied to, if they are not flogged for their lack of faith, if they are assured that nothing can separate them from the love of God, then there is no reason for them to be damaged by prayer. What it finally comes down to is that people do not regret being loved by God and his people. The very worst that can happen when we pray is that nothing will happen. As pastor and theologian Ray Anderson summarizes,

> This means that one who practices the art of the cure of souls need not possess the omniscience of God himself before daring to take up this ministry. . . . Lacking infallibility, I will sometimes err in discernment and other times fail to act appropriately due to lack of faith. Have I missed a demon somewhere in interpreting aberrant behavior and allowed the person to suffer what should have been cured through exorcism? Probably. Have I stopped short of a miracle of healing? . . . Probably. But not intentionally or perversely, and not in the sense of ultimately dooming myself or the other.[3]

In the last analysis, we do not require certainty that our prayers for healing will work. Nor do we need assurances that offering hope for healing will never disappoint. These concerns, real though they may be, are overridden by the command of Christ to preach the gospel of the kingdom and to heal the sick and cast out demons. The final reason for taking up the ministry of healing is simply out of obedience to Jesus Christ. The ultimate responsibility for the effect of this obedience rests with him.

Whether or not we obey him, however, is not a matter of indifference to him. In Luke 10:17-21, the seventy-two return to Jesus full of joy because, as they exclaim, "Even the demons submit to us in your name." Jesus is caught up in the festive mood and, "full of joy through the Holy Spirit," he praises the Father. Jesus rejoices when we accept and respond to the implications of his kingship.

This proclamation and demonstration not only brings our Lord and Savior joy, but it is also part God's plan for the ultimate salvation and re-creation of the world. In Matthew 24:14, Jesus asserts, "This gospel of the kingdom will be preached in the whole world as a testimony to all nations, and then the end will come."

What Jesus means by "this gospel of the kingdom" is the same gospel he preached for three years. The only gospel of the kingdom Jesus speaks of is that gospel which proclaims the good news of reconciliation while demonstrating that good news in healing and deliverance. We are called by Christ to participate in the adventure of the whole gospel. There is no reason not to expect victory as we preach and do this gospel. The power of evil in all its expressions will shatter. The gates of hell will fall before the advance of this gospel (Mt 16:18).

In witnessing the effects of this whole gospel around the world and seeing it manifest more and more in our midst, it becomes realistic to expect that we actually might preach the good news to the entire world in our generation. George Ladd exhorts us to this adventure and reassures us as we go:

> The kingdom of God has attacked the kingdom of Satan; this evil age has been assaulted by the age to come in the person of Christ. All authority is now his. He will not display this authority in its final glorious victory until he comes again but the authority is now his. Satan is defeated and bound; death is conquered; sin is broken. All authority is his. "Go you therefore."[4]

Amen!

PART III

BEGINNING A HEALING MINISTRY

THE CHRISTIAN COMMUNITY IS GIVEN TO THE world as a sign of the kingdom of God. Not least among the signs we are to show to the world is healing the sick. We have seen that Jesus' ministry had two foci—preaching and healing. He intends that his followers continue this word-work ministry. After his resurrection, Jesus said to them, "As the Father has sent me, I am sending you" (Jn 20:21). Earlier he had told them, "As you go, preach this message: 'The kingdom of heaven is near.' Heal the sick . . ." (Mt 10:7-8). And when he had sent out the seventy-two, he commanded them to "Heal the sick . . . and tell them, 'The kingdom of God is near you' " (Lk 10:9).

We have already seen how certain ways of thinking discourage would-be healers from doing all that Christ called us to do. But now that we have developed a theology which supports a healing ministry, we still need practical know-how. In addition to clear biblical thinking, we need to learn from pastoral experience. The five-pronged model which I present in this section is especially designed to help Christian groups with little or no experience in healing the sick to get started in this ministry.

CHAPTER TEN

MODELS OF HEALING

As WE HAVE SEEN, EVANGELICAL THEOLOGY PROVIDES US WITH a solid foundation for a ministry of healing. The question now is, How do we carry on such ministry? Most evangelicals involved in healing and deliverance today do not operate with models of ministry from within their own tradition. The majority of us have learned to heal the sick and demonized from people in other traditions, and we have adopted their styles and procedures in the process.

This is not necessarily wrong in itself, but I am persuaded that we would be much more effective and create less dissension in this work if our models of healing arose out of our theological convictions and everyday church life. C. Peter Wagner, a missiologist and church growth expert, recently wrote:

I can't recall meeting an evangelical pastor who does not believe in divine healing. In the average midweek prayer meeting, long lists of sick people requesting prayers for healing are common. James 5, where some instructions are given for praying for the sick, is in the Canon. Most pastors can point to patients they prayed for who were healed. Why then do relatively few evangelical churches carry on a regular ministry of healing?[1]

Wagner answers his own question, noting that the polarization and division which often result when healing ministries are introduced are the prime reason that more churches do not have them. Tensions, he explains, might be avoided if individual churches developed healing ministry models which are in harmony with their own theological values and church life.

Time and again churches have polarized because they imported forms of ministry which were helpful elsewhere but inappropriate for themselves. Understandably, the healing ministry of Jesus has taken different shapes and forms among various traditions. We should value this and also remember that even though we agree fully on the aims of a particular ministry, we may differ widely on the means.

Generally speaking, a healing ministry model ought to evolve naturally in a local church rather than being imposed. A ministry which grows out of a church's theological values and body life will carry with it the mother church's genetic code, so to speak. Therefore, it will fit more easily alongside other ministries birthed by this church. As a naturally conceived and delivered child, it is more likely to be accepted by the rest of the church family and less likely to offend.

This is not to suggest that a congregation that wants to develop a healing ministry must start from scratch. On the contrary, we can learn much from what God has taught the church over the years. I am merely cautioning against the all-too-prevalent practice of churches imposing on themselves a valid ministry in a form which is alien to them.

New Testament Models of Healing

In thinking through what form a ministry of healing and deliverance might take in my own and other mainstream evangelical churches, I first consulted the New Testament. Scripture provides a norm not only for what we believe but also for how we act, including how we practice Christ's ministry of healing.

In reading the New Testament, I was initially disturbed to see that Jesus healed the sick and cast out demons very differently from the way we do it today. Every healing ministry I am familiar with depends largely on prayer. Jesus healed primarily by command. Unlike his followers today, he did not petition for healing; he pronounced it. "When evening came, many who were demon-possessed were brought to him, and he drove out the spirits with a word and healed all the sick" (Mt 8:16). He healed a leper by saying, "Be clean!" (Mk 1:41). He raised a dead girl by saying, "Get up!" (Mk 5:41). On occasion I have observed people pronounce healing in Jesus' name with dramatic success, but I know of no one today who consistently and effectively follows Jesus' pattern.

At the close of his earthly ministry Jesus told the church, "Anyone who has faith in me will do what I have been doing. He will do even greater things than these, because I am going to the Father" (Jn 14:12). The early church did do the works of Christ, but as we shall see it did them differently than he.

At times, a command in the name of Jesus was sufficient for healing (Acts 3:6), but beginning in the book of Acts, we find prayer to be the church's general method of healing. Peter prayed for Tabitha in Acts 9:40. Paul prayed before healing the father of Publius in Acts 28:8.

James also notes that if someone is sick they are to call for the elders of the church. Those elders are to pray in the name of the Lord, and the prayer of faith will heal the sick person (Jas 5:14-15).

From its earliest days until now, prayer has been essential to the healing ministry of the church. Thus in developing healing models within the evangelical mainstream, we should expect prayer in Jesus' name to be central.

Traits Common to All Healing Traditions

After analyzing the form and structure of various healing models in Scripture, I reviewed the healing ministry in some traditions where it is already established, for example, Anglican-Episcopal, Pentecostal, Lutheran, Roman Catholic, Greek Orthodox and various independent charismatic groups. I was especially interested to discover what elements of style, if any, were common to ministries of healing throughout today's church. I assumed that if there were techniques and procedures which were shared by all these parts of the body of Christ, they could be embraced by the rest of us as well. What I learned from this study was at times puzzling but for the most part very instructive and encouraging.[2]

In examining the healing models within the church today, I found no structural or procedural elements common to all. Each tradition has a model of ministry which reflects its own history and theological ideals. It was liberating for me to discover that God works through the peculiar character and beliefs of each group to facilitate healing and deliverance. In developing our own healing models, we need not feel pressured to conform to techniques or expectations of other groups nor should we sit in judgment on them. Particular methods of healing are not essential in themselves but rather appropriate or inappropriate, depending on their context. There are, however, certain common values and attitudes which inform and empower each of them.

One assumption shared by all Christians who participate in vital healing ministries is that God wills to heal the sick, that he desires wholeness rather than sickness for his people. Those who are consistently effective in praying for the sick anticipate healing. I discussed and affirmed this at length in chapter five.

The second cardinal element present among healing communities is a sincere compassion for those in pain. Or we could say that there is always a participation in Jesus' compassion. Whether you are present with an Orthodox priest as he offers up the Eucharist or with a Pentecostal healer as she reaches out to touch the bent limb, you detect human compassion for other humans. Whether you are in London at an Anglican healing service or in San Antonio at a Catholic deliverance Mass or in Detroit at a charismatic prayer group or in Anaheim at a Vineyard Christian Fellowship healing seminar, you are aware of the participants' concern for sick people.

The third essential element mutually held by Christian groups which effectively pray for the sick is the personal investment and risk-taking of those who pray. Human compassion and belief that God wills healing are fused with a readiness to be vulnerable in the attempt to heal. Jim Glennon once said to me: "In the past twenty-five years of praying for the sick, I have felt that I was at once on the brink of disaster and on the verge of a miracle." This risk-taking comes in many forms, but it is always present among groups who are proficient in healing. I will discuss this further in chapter thirteen.

Christian healing is a mystery which cannot be controlled by applying some cause-and-effect formula. Those who pray for the sick enter an unseen world of spiritual forces which cannot be fully comprehended. It is at once fellowship with God in his work and warfare against the lawless destruction of evil. Those who risk entering this realm expose themselves and the ones they pray for to the possibility of humiliation and defeat without ever knowing why. This personal investment, which I label faith, is present in all healing ministries.

In fashioning healing ministries which are compatible with our own theological convictions and church life, we need not feel pressed to conform to any particular model. Neither Scripture nor the church at large has decreed particular structural or procedural elements to be essential. The Bible and the body of Christ, however, have revealed that at the heart of the Christian healing ministry are the above-mentioned values which will inform our healing models regardless of the forms they take.

CHAPTER ELEVEN

GETTING STARTED

THE HEALING MODEL THAT I DISCUSS IN THIS CHAPTER I learned from John Wimber at Fuller Theological Seminary.[1] Baptist, Pentecostal, Lutheran, Presbyterian, Methodist, Missionary Alliance and Independent church leaders were all in the class. None of them voiced any objection to it, most became proficient in its use, and some in turn taught it to their congregations. The model travels well among various traditions and is easily taught, comprehended and practiced. It is particularly well suited for those who have little or no background in healing the sick. It gets people involved in ministry immediately at a comfortable level, and it tells them where to start and when to stop.

The five steps in this ministry model are (1) interviewing, (2) choosing a prayer strategy, (3) praying for specific results, (4) assessing the results and (5) giving postprayer direction.

Interviewing

The first step is to interview the person in need. The purpose at this stage is simply to gather pertinent information. The information may be anything from finding out where it hurts to reviewing the individual's family history.

A variety of questions can be used to begin the interview. When did the problem start? Who besides you reacts to it? How have you dealt with this problem in the past? Has anyone tried to help you with this concern before? Do you know the cause of your sickness or pain? Do you see sin or relational stress contributing to it? What changes in your life will occur if you are healed?

Open-ended questions such as these encourage the person's participation in the process and enables the gathering of helpful information.

As people give their own report of the problem, learn to listen between the lines. Hurting persons may know more about their problems than they are willing to say, or they may be unaware of the underlying causes which nonetheless may be detected by the skilled listener.

In addition to listening intently to the person, learn to listen to God. The Good Shepherd knows his sheep and desires to help us help them. He may, therefore, at any moment communicate to us something vital about a person that will assist in the healing process.

This kind of on-the-spot communication is generally referred to as a "word of knowledge" or a "word of insight." These words or communications come in various forms and, if we are expectant and open, we may learn to receive them.

Spiritual insights sometime come in the form of mental pictures. These images may be literal—like pictures of the damaged part of the person's body—or they may be symbolic, revealing the underlying spiritual, relational or emotional cause of the problem.

I was once praying for a man who asked for help because of chest pain which he assumed was heart trouble. As I prayed over him, I saw in my mind a line drawing of a person's stomach. At the top of the stomach was an angry red ulcer. I told him what I saw. I then shifted my prayer from his heart to his stomach, and the pain left immediately. A week later, he had a medical checkup at my request. The exam confirmed that his stomach and not his heart had been the problem.

On another occasion, I prayed over a woman who suffered from a host of stress-related ailments. She was chronically tired and was in constant pain because of muscle tension. I thought that if we could deal with the source of the stress, we could more effectively pray for healing. When I asked her what the stress was, she said she didn't know. Then in my mind I saw this woman sitting in the corner of a room, tears streaming down her face, holding a broken doll. I asked her if she had ever had an abortion. She stared back at me, wide-eyed, and whispered, "My husband doesn't even know about it." After a time of confession and receiving God's forgiveness, her pain left and her energy returned. She has been fine ever since.

A word of knowledge or insight may also come through a word or phrase "seen" or "heard" in the listener's mind. Sometimes insight into a person's need comes by way of an immediate and definite conviction. The person praying may just come to know something to be true without knowing why or how.

These then seem to be some of the more common means by which God facilitates healing through what we call the word of knowledge. As in other spiritual skills, hearing from God in this way and discerning what is from God and what is not comes through trial and error and honest feedback from others. This kind of discernment, like all others, is the daughter of experience.

In conducting the interview, avoid getting caught up in a medical analysis of the problem. The medical history of the sickness is probably of value only to a physician. The purpose of the interview is to determine as closely as possible the cause of the condition—natural, spiritual, relational, emotional—so that the one who prays can do so specifically.

That is not to suggest that the interview is only a preliminary exercise or merely a means to an end. Depending on how the interview is conducted, it may in itself have profound healing value. All counselors know that effective listening is healing. Intense listening is indistinguishable from love, and love heals.

This kind of listening means that the people receiving attention are allowed to be the experts on their own pain. They are also cared for as total persons. This is to say, their personhood is central, not their sickness. This kind of listening not only builds up and heals, it also encourages people in need toward deeper self-disclosure through increased trust. It is usually at the deep layers of personality that the roots of the sickness may be found. Listeners then must be persons worthy of trust. Minister are servants and must be committed to the best interests of those seeking help, recognizing that Jesus calls us to serve each other out of our shared humanity.

While posturing and manipulating are always wrong, this does not mean that our ministry is to be nondirective. God really has authorized and equipped us to heal in his name, and there will come times to exercise his authority decisively.

The interview is complete when you believe you understand enough about the problem—its origin, history, scope and significance—to go about choosing a prayer strategy.

Choosing a Prayer Strategy

The interview provides some idea of the nature and cause of the sickness, and this in turn determines how we pray. Let me stress from the outset that since we are complex beings, sickness of any kind cannot always be diagnosed simply. The symptoms of physical illness and mental disturbance are usually rooted in spiritual, emotional and relational causes that are not obvious at first.

Paul Tournier, the famous Swiss physician, explained a truth years ago that many of us are discovering for ourselves as we pray for the sick. The thesis of his book *The Healing of Persons* is that spiritual unrest, emotional trauma and damaged relationships underlie most chronic and serious illnesses.[2] Similarly, Dr. Robert M. Cunningham of the Mayo Clinic notes:

Four out of five times I'd find out what was wrong sooner if I started by examining the patient's home life, his job and his bank account instead of his heart, his digestive system and his kidneys.[3]

In a systematic, scientifically controlled study at the Cancer Counseling and Research Center in Dallas, Texas, Dr. O. Carl Simonton demonstrated the significant cause-and-effect relationship between emotional stress and the onset of many types of cancer.[4]

Much of the literature dealing with the relationship of states of mind to physical illness agrees that there is a high correlation between mental stress and what we call chronic illness. The consensus is that virtually every headache, the vast majority of gastric disorders, most skin diseases, allergies, asthma and lower back pain are caused by unhealthy states of mind—anxiety, guilt, bitterness, and such. The Bible makes frequent mention of the relationship of body to mind and spirit as in Psalms 62, 31:10, 38:3, Proverbs 3:5-8, 14:30 and 17:22.

Some time ago, a young woman came to be prayed for regarding a host of physical ailments. During the interview she disclosed that she had spent years on the street working as a prostitute. We prayed for her repeatedly over several weeks and were ineffective in healing her physically. After awhile we began to realize that many of her sicknesses were rooted in the guilt she felt because of her past life. We shifted our attention from her physical problems to her spiritual need for repentance and forgiveness. After several more meetings, she began to experience God's forgiveness and was substantially healed physically as a result.

Sin affects not only the health of the person who sins but also the health of those sinned against. Often a person who has been abused as a child, a girl or boy who is raped, a husband who is betrayed by his wife, or a wife who is beaten by her husband may develop chronic physical illnesses as a result.

Our health is deeply affected by how we react to sins committed against us. Resentment, bitterness and hate all hurt and often disable those in whom they take root. I recently prayed over a woman with a bleeding ulcer, who was not healed until she forgave her father for sexually abusing her. Another man was healed of arthritis only after he forgave his boss for betraying him. A rape victim was not freed from crippling compulsive fear until she forgave the men who assaulted her. Learning to forgive others is often the key which unlocks the door leading to restoration and health.

The causes of some sicknesses are not easily determined. They may stem from broken relationships or vague, ill-defined inner conflicts such as self-doubt and feelings of insignificance. These and numerous other nonorganic disorders may bring on the symptoms of physical disease.

Other physical and emotional sickness may be caused by the demonic. The New Testament and experience in praying for the sick show that demons cause some illnesses which cannot be cured until the demons are expelled.

These, then, are but a few of the possible underlying causes of sickness. Sick or hurting people may or may not understand the origins of their pain, but whenever possible these root causes should be got at so that counsel and prayer may be specific and therefore more effective.

Not every sickness is necessarily rooted in some psychological or spiritual disorder. An illness or pain may have no more significance than that we live in a fallen world which is prone to disease at every level. We then simply pray that the problem be corrected without searching for any significance behind it. But the effort to discern root causes is important, since for reasons that are not self-evident, the more specific we are in prayer, the more effective we are in healing sickness.

Praying for Specific Results

Praying for specific, measurable results is also important. When we pray against pain, for instance, we ought to monitor the increase or decrease of that specific pain. As we pray over someone with arthritis, we should stop periodically to check the swelling and range of movement in the affected joints. If we pray for someone with asthma, we should listen for improvement in breathing. When the problem, like cancer or diabetes, is hidden and not easily monitored, we should encourage the person to consult a doctor as soon as possible to determine what, if anything, is happening.

Praying for specific results requires us to press for things that are observable and measurable. In order to determine results, we seek honest and accurate feedback. In this kind of praying, we keep our eyes, ears and minds open in order to observe the specific consequences of our praying. This approach revolutionizes the prayer lives of many who have been conditioned to pray in a vague, nondirective fashion.

When we pray for specific results, we do so based on the revealed will of God in Scripture, empowered and guided by the Holy Spirit. By remaining critically aware, we are better able to "see what the Father is doing" and therefore we become more fit to cooperate with him in his work.

When Christians are prayed over for healing, there is often implicit and sometimes explicit pressure placed on them to report improvement when there is none. This distortion of reality is often the result of some form of wishful thinking. Or it may spring from a desire to make God or the minister look good. In other circumstances, this tendency to say things are happening in healing when they are not results from an overzealous approach to faith. Regardless of the cause, any claiming of healing which has not occurred, or denying of symptoms which in fact exist, is not only dishonest but also dangerous. We have discussed some of the theological and psychological dangers of this approach already in chapter three.

Another practical danger is that if the people praying do not get an accurate report on progress, their potentially effective ministry may be frustrated. When those who pray for the sick are misled into believing that a particular approach to a problem is helping when it is not, they may continue down an unfruitful path and therefore miss one which would have yielded better results. What may also be missed is some specific truth which God is seeking to communicate at the time.

Another danger of inaccurate feedback while praying for the sick is that spiritual or medical help may be stopped short of bringing about a true cure. Many of the dangers inherent in lying to a medical doctor about the status of a disease apply to the ministry of Christian healing as well. Distortions and illusions are of no help to the healing ministry of the church. Nothing positive is ever gained through deception. God is committed to what is real, and it is through reality at all levels that his grace comes to us.

The value of accurate feedback from people we pray for is illustrated by the healing ministry of Jesus. The blind man whom Jesus healed at Bethsaida was not cured instantly. Jesus stopped at one point in the healing process to ask if the blind man could see anything yet. The man looked up and said, "I see people; they look like trees walking around" (Mk 8:24). From this accurate feedback Jesus knew that sight was not completely restored but that it was improving. So Jesus put his hands on the man's eyes again and completed his work.

Jesus never counseled anyone to claim a healing which had not occurred, nor did he ever ask sick people to deny their symptoms. People were either healed or they were not. As we follow Jesus in his ministry to the sick and demonized, nothing will be gained by distorting reality.

In praying for specific results, we expect something to happen and so we look for it. As a result of training and firsthand experience, we will learn better how to interpret what we observe.

The responsibility of listening intently during the interview, diagnosing the problem correctly, choosing an appropriate prayer strategy and then praying for measurable results is intimidating for some people. Don't let the challenge or the mechanics of ministry bog you down. After all, it's not our character or any technique which heals. We are only junior partners in this ministry. It is God who heals— he takes ultimate responsibility. And he so desires to heal people that he will often find a way to do so despite you.

The worst that can happen when you lovingly pray for someone is that nothing will happen. People are remarkably tolerant and even appreciative of any attempt to help them so long as it is made with care and respect.

Frederick Buechner offers some lighthearted and practical advice for would-be healers. While praying for the sick, he says,

> if you feel like a fool as you are doing this, don't let it throw you. You are a fool of course. . . . Don't try too hard to feel religious, to generate some healing power of your own. Think of yourself rather (if you have to think of yourself at all) as a rather small-gauge, clogged-up pipe that a little of God's power may be able to filter through if you can just stay loose enough. Tell the one you are praying for to stay loose too.[5]

Assessing the Results

After a time of listening and praying, we must honestly analyze what has happened. If healing is complete, then obviously those involved can stop and give thanks. If healing has only begun, which is most often the case, then prayer may be continued or another appointment may be scheduled.

If little or no healing appears to have occurred, the diagnosis may be in error and further interviewing may be necessary to gather more or better information. Or it may be necessary to concede defeat for the moment and allow some time for reflection to pass.

A young woman I will call Helen, who happened to be a registered nurse, attended a healing conference I conducted. She admitted being very skeptical of divine healing because of her medical knowledge. Nevertheless she decided in the end to ask for prayer for herself.

Helen was born with a form of spina bifida which left the vertebrae in her lower back deformed. One leg was significantly shorter than the other, and the foot on that leg turned in. She limped as a result.

After a time of prayer, we assessed her condition. Nothing had happened so far as we could see. She told me later that, although nothing physically happened to her, the first time we prayed she was spiritually changed. She explained that somehow hope sprang up in her heart. She felt sure that she would be healed sometime in the future.

Four months after that initial encounter, she came to another healing conference and when I asked for those with one leg shorter than the other to come up for prayer, Helen responded immediately. After we prayed for a few seconds, her short leg grew out even with the other. Needless to say, we were excited and pleased for her, but, as part of our honest assessment, we had to say that the foot on the once-too-short leg was still turned in. Her healing was not complete. She told us not to be concerned. She believed the Lord would do the rest too—the next evening he did.

Sometime during a three-hour prayer session with some of her friends the following night, Helen's foot straightened out. When she got up to walk on it, she was alarmed because her gate felt awkward. Her friends laughed and said, "That's because you don't limp any more."

Rigorous, honest assessment of the results of our prayer is necessary and helpful, but never complete. With God involved, there is always more going on than meets the eye. His love and power revealed in Jesus Christ means that optimism is always appropriate.

Giving Postprayer Direction

It may be necessary to counsel people after we have prayed for them. More often than not, healing is gradual, unlike most healings performed by Jesus and the apostles. From what we see in the text of the New Testament, the majority of the healings recorded there were instantaneous. Notable exceptions to this are the progressive healing of the blind man at Bethsaida (Mk 8:22-25) and the delayed healings of the ten lepers (Lk 17:14).

Some healings today are instantaneous and dramatic. For the most part, however, the symptoms associated with illness or injury disappear progressively. Once healing has begun, this process will be helped or hindered by the thoughts and actions of the person being healed. Good counsel and support at these levels are essential.

People ill because of anxiety, for instance, will not progress as they should if they remain anxious. A close friend of mine suffered serious lower back pain for years due to stress. On three occasions, he was prayed over by friends who were experienced in healing prayer. On each occasion, he reported significant improvement regarding his symptoms. The pain in his back was dramatically relieved, and his range of movement was all but restored. In a matter of three to five days, however, his symptoms returned in full force.

Only after my friend came to a deeper understanding of the root of his anxiety and how to appropriate God's grace in dealing with it did his back finally remain healed. The spasms in the muscles of his back were in fact released through prayer. The habitual anxiety which caused them to return, however, was healed only as he changed his destructive thinking.

Another friend of mine had a man in his congregation who had been out of work for seven years because of severe arthritis. After repeated prayer for healing, the man received almost total relief from his crippling pain. He was then confronted with having to return to work after many years off. As the day for him to go out job-hunting approached, his pain returned. Not until he was helped over his anxiety about returning to work did his healing last.

Some sickness is caused by sin, and in such cases we cannot expect healing to be significant or permanent unless that sin is repented of. The counseling and support following prayer in such cases should be directed toward this end. For instance, people who are sick due to the abuse of drugs or alcohol can expect no permanent healing through prayer till they stop their abuse. In such cases, the cause and effect of sin and sickness and the need for postprayer direction is obvious, but this connection is not always so apparent.

A young woman once asked me for prayer regarding swelling and severe pain in her abdomen. She reported her doctors could find no cause for the symptoms and therefore could prescribe no treatment. As a group of us prayed for her, the swelling and pain disappeared. She left the meeting rejoicing but returned the next week with the same symptoms. We prayed again with the same result, but a week later she was back again painfully swollen.

We were obviously not reaching the root of her problem, so I asked her if there was some significant sin in her life connected to her sickness. After some hesitation she confessed that she was secretly engaged in a homosexual relationship. The connection between her sin and sickness was not apparent to her or to us, but in the week following, with our help, she broke off the sinful relationship and received permanent healing for her body.

This young woman illustrates again that it is persons who are sick and not merely their bodies. Postprayer direction addresses the needs and the responsibilities of the whole person. On occasion, we must say to people, "Go and sin no more." In the case of sin-related sickness, church discipline becomes a critical element in the healing process.[6]

The need for postprayer direction is most essential in cases of deliverance. Jesus explained that when an evil spirit is driven out, it may return in force if not prevented from doing so (Mt 12:43-45). Simply because a person is delivered of evil spirits does not imply that healing is permanent. Often without a change in lifestyle and patterns of thought, "the final condition of that man is worse than the first" (Mt 12:45). Ongoing pastoral care by skilled helpers and the person's involvement in a small group may be part of the post-prayer direction.

Yet another postprayer directive might be, "Keep on praying!" A mother of two young children recently came to one of our healing seminars asking for prayer. She had what doctors referred to as inoperable, terminal cancer. She had six months to live.

This young woman was raised in a Christian home and had developed a disciplined prayer life. When we first met her, she and her friends had been praying for her regularly for several months. Her condition worsened during this time, but she refused to quit praying or to allow anyone else to quit.

We joined in the stream of persistent prayer for her that evening she came to us. The next morning she went for her weekly exam and "regress" report. To the amazement of the four specialists examining her, she was now in rapid remission. There was no medical explanation for what they saw. The cancerous tumor which for months had been consuming her body at an accelerating rate had now all but disappeared. Weeks later I received a report that she had made a complete recovery.

Until three years ago I suffered constant pain in my lower back. After accepting the reality that God wanted to heal me, I asked for help. When I was prayed for, it seemed to respond only slightly. I asked my wife, Patti, and my friend John White to pray for me five minutes a day until the problem cleared up. They agreed to. Patti prayed five minutes in the evening and John prayed five minutes at noon over lunch. In four months the pain was gone and has never returned.

Postprayer counsel may take various forms, depending on the needs of the person, the resources of the community and the spiritual discernment of those who minister. It is an important aspect of the healing ministry and may make the difference in its effectiveness.

Learn by Doing

The five-step model of Christian healing that I have outlined here is not all that can be said about healing. But it has proven to be an excellent model for getting people and churches with little experience started in healing the sick.

The model travels well and may be used in one-on-one situations as well as in small groups and conference settings. With specific contextual adaptations, it fits into the church life of most Christian communities.

Training people in the healing ministry with the use of this model may be done in small groups or in larger settings. Those with some experience should teach and illustrate it. If no experienced person can be found, resource people suitable to the group should be brought in as trainers.

The components of training should include instruction, modeling, practice, feedback and more practice. Care should be taken not to allow this training model to be presented as instruction only. No Christian ministry, including the ministry of healing, can be learned except by doing it.

The disciples learned the ministry of healing by listening to Jesus' instruction, by watching him heal the sick and cast out demons, and finally by doing it themselves (Lk 10). These followers of Jesus in turn taught others by the same method. Soon the entire world knew about the healing power and authority of Christ. By this same method, the ministry of healing is being returned to the church and spread abroad in the world today.

CHAPTER TWELVE

WHOLENESS AND HEALING IN THREE DIMENSIONS

IN DISCUSSING HOW TO PRAY FOR THE SICK IN THE PREVIOUS chapter we noted the complex nature of much illness and how the root of an illness may be hidden. I want now to follow up on this observation by discussing the mind, the spirit and the body, and how they interact in sickness and healing. Let me say at the outset that this discussion is meant to help clarify and simplify prayer, not clutter and complicate it. This information should enable our praying for the sick to be better informed, more precise and therefore more effective.

The first principle to have firmly in our thinking is that mind, spirit and body are not precisely defined separate categories. They are, rather, imprecise but convenient labels to describe the components of human nature.

The Bible views the human being holistically. It sees the person as a single entity. The Old Testament, for instance, does not have a word for what we call "body" as distinguished from "mind" and "spirit." The biblical writers did not think of the body as having a reality or status of its own. In biblical Hebrew there are over eighty names for body parts (hand, eye, foot, and so forth) but no names for the sum of these parts. The word which comes closest to denoting what we call "body" is *basar,* but it refers to the total life of a person. Therefore, the idea of disease as strictly physical is unknown in Scripture.

Unlike Old Testament Hebrew, New Testament Greek does have a word for the physical body—*soma.* But unlike Greek philosophy, the New Testament does not view the body as unimportant, evil, or separated from mind and spirit. Our bodies are so valued in the New Testament that we are seen as naked when temporarily separated from them in death. They are so essential to us that God will one day resurrect and perfect them. Jesus who went before us already has his resurrected body, which is the model of what we will be given (Rom 6:5; 1 Cor 15:20, 49; Phil 3:20-21).

Our present corruptible bodies must die to make way for bodies which will never die. Nevertheless the bodies we have today, along with our minds and spirits, are objects of God's love and saving power.[1] The term "salvation" itself is interchangeable with the term "healing" in the New Testament. This is why one Greek word so frequently applies to physical as well as spiritual healing (Mt 9:21; Mk 5:23· Lk 7:50).

So the Bible views the human being as a single integrated entity and the healing of the human being as comprehensive. While keeping this holistic perspective in mind, we must also distinguish the various aspects of human nature while praying for the sick.

Discovering how sickness and sin attack us at various levels and seeing how these levels interact to spread the effects of sin and sickness helps us as we pray for healing. A human being is a kind of ecosystem, a complex and interdependent whole. Pollution in one part contaminates all, and dealing with the pollution at its source heals all. I am indebted to Professor Peter Davids for many of the theological and psychological insights which inform the following discussion of mind, spirit and body.[2]

Mind

What I label "mind" is also referred to in Scripture as "heart" or "soul." It is the area of thought, emotion and will. Our emotions become sick and our wills become weak when we feed our minds distortions. If we understand life to be meaningless, for instance, our thinking in general becomes sick, and we fall prey to other cognitive distortions.

If we pollute our minds with moral filth and pornographic images, we become emotional and volitional cripples who are incapable of distinguishing between good and evil, beauty and ugliness, love and lust. Jesus devoted a great deal of time and energy to diagnosing the mind sicknesses of his religious contemporaries—pride, legalism and hypocrisy. He also prescribed the cure—repentance!

Some illnesses of the mind are not chosen but inflicted. Early-childhood rejection, for instance, sets up in our thinking a wrong view of ourselves, the world and even God. If such distortions are not discerned and dealt with, our minds will never function in the healthy way God intended them to.

Spirit

What I call "spirit" is that invisible part of us which touches and relates to God and other spirits. Some of the spiritual forces around us are good (the Holy Spirit and holy angels). Some spiritual forces are evil (Satan, demons, principalities and powers). These evil realities can touch our spirits making them sick. We can be seduced, tormented and even controlled to some degree, through spiritual evil.

Spiritual sickness may come if we habitually sin or rebel against God and thereby invite evil to draw near us. Spiritual sickness may begin by seeking occult experiences. Or it may come unbidden through a trauma or a curse. Such sickness must be properly diagnosed and effectively dealt with through our own spiritual openness to the delivering power of God's Holy Spirit.

Body

What I refer to as "body" is the visible and most obvious part of our being. Our bodies are the means by which we affect the physical world and the means by which the physical world affects us.

There are, of course, many ways our bodies become damaged and sick. Wounds caused by accidents, stress of various kinds and disease may leave our bodies chronically sick.

Jesus healed such damaged bodies during his ministry, and he calls us to do the same in his name. When it appears that the sickness we are dealing with is confined to the physical plane, we should pray over it simply and confidently.

Diseases are often interrelated, the cure of one bringing about the cure of others. Several months ago I was approached by a woman named Lynn and her doctor, who both wanted prayer for her diabetes. Lynn's doctor was a competent physician who also knew how to pray for the sick, so I felt no inclination to ask her questions or search for any nonphysical root to her disease. I simply prayed that God would heal her diabetes.

The next morning Lynn tested her blood sugar (she had been insulin dependent for several years). That morning, for the first time in a very long time, her blood-sugar level was normal. A week later she had a comprehensive exam which revealed that, in addition to normal blood sugar, her blood pressure for the first time in years was also normal. Months later her blood sugar and pressure are still normal, and she is steadily loosing her excess weight. One part of her physical organism affected all of it, and when that one part was healed, healing spread to the rest as well.

Healing and Sickness Interactions

Just as diseases may be interrelated at the physical level, they may also be affected by interactions between the planes of human nature. We will now look at a few representative interactions among the mind, spirit and body to see how understanding these interactions may help us to bring about healing.

Mind-Spirit. Strictly speaking, our minds are neither spiritual nor physical, yet a sick mind will affect these areas too. People who nurse bitterness in their mind (heart, soul) and refuse to forgive others will soon become sick spiritually and physically.

According to the New Testament, the one who does not forgive is cut off from God's forgiveness (Mt 6:12-15; Mk 11:25-26; Lk 6:37). This makes the person spiritually sick.

Another sickness of the mind occurs when it affirms a distorted concept of God. This will in time seep into the spiritual life and pollute it. Heretics begin their spiritual alienation from the One True God by thinking wrongly about him.

A less obvious mental sickness which nevertheless infects spiritual life is a wrong view of God held by many orthodox believers—the view that God is distant, uncaring and unfeeling. The person who sees God this way is functionally cut off from much of the Father's love and power. A sick mind makes the spirit dysfunctional, and it is helpful to discern this connection when it exists.

Mind-Body. Almost everyone these days recognizes that the mind dramatically affects the body. Most people are well aware of recent discoveries in the field of psychosomatic medicine. Bitterness which begins in the mind, for instance, not only makes the spirit sick but will in time affect the body. Arthritis, ulcers, cancer and a host of other physical ailments can often be traced back to a bitter attitude of mind. Until the mind is healed of its sin-sickness, physical healing is unlikely. And should healing occur apart from repentance, it will not last.

Spirit-Mind. A sick spirit can damage an otherwise healthy mind. A state of spiritual alienation from God and the objective guilt that is a part of that state may cause anxiety and stress in a person's mind. Pop psychology and pop religion may try hard to mask these feelings of anxiety with positive affirmation and other mental anesthetics. But true healers will discern the root cause and, instead of praying against the emotional symptoms, they will prescribe repentance and faith.

A person's spirit can be made sick by other spirits as well as by its own objective guilt. The human spirit, as that part of us which relates to other spirits, can be affected by unclean ones. When our spirits are contacted by evil, they distort our thinking and cause emotional pain. Again, it is useful in the healing ministry to detect these interactions. Good information and skilled counseling are not sufficient to heal sick thinking if it stems from a demonically oppressed spirit.

Spirit-Body. Spiritual sin-sickness will in turn hurt a person's body. Spiritual alienation from God often produces anxiety in the mind, and this in turn damages the body. David was only too aware of the spirit-body interaction in producing sickness when he wrote, "My bones wasted away through my groaning all day long. For day and night your hand was heavy upon me; my strength was sapped" (Ps 32:3-4).

There is also the more direct and obvious connection between spiritual sin and sickness in the case of sexually transmitted diseases. As I noted earlier the human being is a kind of eco-system. Pollution in one part of the system affects the whole.

Body-Mind. A person's mind may be inexplicably filled with anxiety such that he or she is unable to eat or sleep. A medical examiner may discover a brain tumor or a malfunctioning adrenal or thyroid gland as being the cause. When this is the case, no amount of inner-healing or good counsel would make the problem go away. What may appear as a spiritual or psychological problem will not be cleared up unless the physical root is first discerned and dealt with.

Body-Spirit. Our bodies also affect us spiritually. When we are depressed because our supply of adrenalin is low, we tend to be less vital spiritually, prayer is painful, reading and believing the Bible is difficult. What feels like a spiritual problem is really caused by an imbalance in body chemistry.

While making too strict a distinction among mind, spirit and body is biblically questionable, understanding their influences on one another is invaluable in praying for the sick. Discerning separate influences, however, is not a simple task; we are dealing with a magnificently complex ecosystem. Though we have already identified six possible interactions, several of these could be going on at once in any given condition.

In Mark 9:14-29, for instance, we see a boy who is "possessed by a spirit," so we know that he is spiritually sick. He is also showing signs of physical sickness. An EEG examination probably would have revealed that the boy was epileptic; so we could say that he was physically sick too. We can safely assume that the child was in great emotional pain as well, so his mind was sick also.

If this boy were to be diagnosed and treated by medical science today, he would no doubt receive drugs to physically control the seizures. He might be psychologically tested and counseled, and this might bring him some emotional relief. But without discerning the demonic root and casting it out, there could be no substantial cure.

Total Care
Healing prayer does not deny the need for physical medical care or for psychological counseling in the process of healing. There is for me no conflict between instantaneous spiritual or physical healing and more prolonged healing through counseling. I have often found both types to be interdependent and complementary in the healing

of the whole person.

When people are delivered of evil spirits, for instance, I have often found that they are so lacking in self-discipline and social skills that they need extensive pastoral care and structured counseling before they can function properly. Demons were just one of their many serious problems. Our wholeness and complexity should argue strongly for a crossdisciplinary approach to healing. My point here is that our total being is affected by the various aspects of who we are. And often, as in the case of the boy in Mark 9, a radical cure cannot occur until the root cause of the sickness is diagnosed and dealt with.

I have a close friend who suffered for years from a serious malfunction in her digestive system—she was physically sick. She had seen many doctors and specialists who diagnosed her disease, but none offered her any hope of a cure. This of course made her emotionally sick.

Two other friends of mine (a husband and wife) discerned, while praying for her, that she was ill because of a voodoo curse placed on her by a witch doctor when she lived in Africa. The couple broke the curse in the name of Jesus, and that night, for the first time in six and a half years, she was able to sleep through till morning. The next day she no longer needed her medication; her digestive system was functioning properly. One year later, she underwent a thorough medical examination, which to the surprise of her doctors, revealed a complete recovery of her digestive functions.

Another friend of mine suffered terribly from asthma—he was physically sick. He was also depressed and anxious much of the time—he was emotionally sick. From time to time he was hospitalized for both physical and mental illnesses but received no lasting help. We prayed for his physical and emotional healing but to no avail. Finally, out of desperation, he confessed that in the second year of his marriage he had committed adultery. At some point during this affair his asthma and depression had started. He had always suspected that there was a connection between his sickness and his sin, but he was too fearful and ashamed to confess it.

A few days after his confession he noticed that he was feeling better emotionally and that he no longer needed his atomizer to breathe. A month after his spiritual healing, his breathing and mental state were back to normal. His spiritual healing gave health to his mind and body as well.

A person's mental, spiritual or physical sickness may also be rooted, not in their own sin, but in someone else's sin against them. Our health is contingent not only on what we are and do but often on what others are and do to us.

Some months ago a woman approached me during a healing seminar wanting help with what she labeled an "emotional problem." She became paralyzed with fear when she was alone. This was especially problematic because of her missionary work which obliged her to sometimes travel by herself.

She claimed to have been a happy, secure, well-adjusted Christian woman until two years previously when she had been raped and beaten in a hotel room. From the time of the assault she said she could feel fear stalking her every hour of the day. She had received expert counseling and group therapy but remained hysterically fearful of being alone. As we prayed for her, we discovered evidence of demonic oppression and commanded the demon to leave. After this deliverance she completely recovered her emotional health and experienced no more fear of being alone.

Apparently a spirit attached itself to her, crippling her with fear as a result of someone else's sin. We should view sickness and health not only in light of our own personal interrelatedness but also in view of our corporate interrelatedness.

I have emphasized the wide range of causes of illness so that we will not adopt a one-dimensional understanding of sickness or absolutize a single approach to healing. Beyond this, I want to stress the importance of thinking clearly and rationally about sickness and healing while being totally open to the Holy Spirit for guidance.

Preventive Medicine

We have caught a glimpse of how our wholeness is profoundly affected by our mental and spiritual health. In light of this, imagine a child growing up in an honest and loving Christian home and being trained to believe and live the biblical faith. In most instances, the child would grow up into a healthy and whole adult and go through life avoiding most illnesses (Prov 3:7-8).

The Christian way (according to Scripture) is, among other things, the ultimate prescription for health and wholeness. The following is a list of seven characteristics of the Christian faith, all of which contribute to health:

1. The gospel of Jesus Christ frees the human being from guilt. This, as we have seen, has a profound affect on health (Ps 103:3-5).

2. The Bible commands us to forgive from our heart. This releases us from the crippling effects of bitterness (Mt 6:12-14; Rom 12:17-21).

3. Christianity teaches us to turn from our own striving and to trust and rest in God's faithfulness and provision. This delivers us from the destructiveness of anxiety (Heb 13:5-6).

4. The true Christian way is one of hard work and recreation, punctuated by periods of rest. This balance of activities contributes greatly to health and wholeness (Ps 127:1-2).

5. The Bible teaches the high value and proper care of the body. The health codes in Leviticus and Deuteronomy predate the modern emphasis on nutrition by thousands of years.

6. Christianity encourages regular Bible reading. A mind saturated in the truths of Scripture becomes strong and is thus enabled to properly govern the rest of the personality (Prov 4:20-23).

7. The true Christian way is the way of joy—the joy of being loved by God, loving and being loved by brothers and sisters, and having

something meaningful to contribute to life. A happy person who is convinced of his or her significance will very likely be a healthy individual.

The greatest contribution to health and wholeness within the Christian community is not ultimately the healing ministry, but rather the preventive medicine of following Jesus. While the ministry of healing is only a part of this full-orbed discipleship, it is essential to it. As we follow Jesus in the way of wholeness, we are ready and willing to restore wholeness to those who have lost it. Full obedience to Christ not only promotes our own health but also works to recreate it in others.

CHAPTER THIRTEEN

OBEDIENCE AND THE AUTHORITY TO HEAL

In THE LAST ANALYSIS, WE HAVE NOT BEEN CALLED TO EX-plain sickness and healing; we have been called to heal the sick. If we never move beyond a discussion of the theology that supports healing and the models of ministry that help facilitate healing to actually praying for it, we will miss one of the profound joys of Christian discipleship. Francis MacNutt, a pioneer in the modern healing movement, puts it poignantly:

> As I experience the paradoxes of the healing ministry, I become more and more aware of the mystery involved. Those who want simple answers and absolute clarity are bound to be disappointed. They will never have the beautiful experience that I have almost every day, of seeing a person touched and healed by God's merciful love.[1]

The Joy of Obedience

The sheer joy of healing the sick in the name of Christ does not ultimately depend on a better theological explanation or a more appropriate model. If healing is contingent on anything human, it is contingent on obedience. As we shall see in a moment, Scripture shows us that the authority and power to do the work of God flows through those who obey the Word of God. One of the most dramatic illustrations of the connection between obedience and authority came to me through a girl named Tammy.

Some time ago I attended a healing seminar led by a friend of mine. He brought with him a team of five people to assist him in praying for the sick. After the teaching portion of the seminar, just prior to the ministry time, my friend asked the members of his team to come forward and introduce themselves. One of these especially caught my attention. She was a girl in her late teens who introduced herself as follows: "Hi, my name is Tammy. I'm a single mother; I have been following Jesus a year now. I work at Sears, and I cast out demons and heal the sick." Then she beamed an open, friendly smile and sat down.

I was so stunned yet intrigued by her forthright, unaffected manner that I made a special effort to observe her during the ministry time. Over the course of the evening, she moved among the crowd, attending to one person after another. She was kind and attentive as she spoke to the people and direct and businesslike when she prayed over them. She lived up to her own billing that evening. She did indeed heal the sick, and some dramatically. And she worked with a grace and authority which impressed me.

After the meeting, I asked her how she, being so young and inexperienced, was able to heal and deliver with such authority. She told me some of her personal history, and as she ended her story, she looked straight into my eyes and said, "I didn't get to be a single mom at age seventeen because I was the most moral person in the world. Jesus loved me anyway. He is the only one who ever really did." She continued, "I just love him back and try to do all he tells me to. Jesus wants me to heal people, so I do. He tells me to in the Bible, and my pastor says it's OK, so I just do it."

God has given her authority in the ministry of healing and deliverance because she obeys him. Driven on by her devotion to Christ and with the support of her pastor, she discovered that as she obeys the commands of Jesus, the authority of God is with her.

Tammy showed me what Jesus meant when he said, "I praise you, Father, Lord of heaven and earth, because you have hidden these things from the wise and learned, and revealed them to little children" (Lk 10:21). This was Jesus' joyous response to the Father when his seventy-two followers returned to him exclaiming, "Lord, even the demons submit to us in your name" (v. 17). Jesus had sent them out to heal the sick and proclaim the kingdom of God, and as they obeyed, they discovered the authority of God was with them.

I have observed that the "little children" like Tammy and "unwise, unlearned" Christians in the Third World frequently exercise God's authority to an astounding degree. Unlike many of us, they seem able to suspend their judgment of what is possible and what is not and simply obey the commands of Scripture. We should not be surprised by the connection we find between obedience and authority since authority connected to a life of obedience is a major motif in Scripture.

Obedience and Authority in the Old Testament

In the beginning, Adam exercised authority over creation. Adam's control of his environment meant that the elements cooperated in bringing forth an abundant harvest for him and his mate, and it also meant that their fellow creatures, including the snake, were subject to them. Even though Adam was less powerful than the elements, the beasts and the angels in his world, he ruled them all because God backed up his administration. Adam's effective exercise of God's authority while being subject to God's authority himself ensured that God's will was done on earth and that health and wholeness reigned.

When Satan was created by God, he was endowed with power much greater than that of humans. Satan's inherent might was vastly superior to Adam's, yet he was prevented from working his destructive will on earth because God's authority was with his obedient servant. So long as Adam obeyed God, Satan's superior power was useless against the man.

Satan, being unable to seize control of the world by brute force, had to seduce Adam into disobedience. As Adam moved out from under God's authority through disobedience, he forfeited his own authority in the process. With no man on earth to exercise God's rule, Satan moved into the vacuum to exercise his own power.

Without real authority, Adam was helpless before the superior power of evil. Where before, the earth yielded an abundance of fruit, after, it brought forth weeds. Before Adam disobeyed, he knew only health and wholeness, physically, spiritually and relationally. After he disobeyed, every level of his being experienced disease, destruction and death. God's order and harmony became Satan's anarchy and discord.

God's kingdom rule, once administered by Adam, was replaced by Satan's pseudokingdom rule, administered through his own minions; thus Paul can refer to him as the "god of this age" (2 Cor 4:4). The Lord did not, however, abandon his plundered planet. He set about to rescue a people out of the world and to retain them in obedience to him so that in time his kingdom rule might once again be established on earth.

Throughout Old Testament history, we catch glimpses of the authority which is restored to humanity as servants of God are found faithful. Noah was given authority to save the human race because he obeyed. Abraham was given authority to father and bless many nations because he obeyed. Moses was given authority to save God's people out of Egypt and to lead them to the land of promise because he obeyed. God's pattern in dealing with people was consistent. He looked for those whom he could train to obey. As they learned obedience, often through what they suffered, they were entrusted with authority and given power to make that authority effective. Throughout Bible history, God made his will known and his rule effective through obedient men and women.

At the same time, the biblical record shows that just as there is a correlation between obedience and authority, so there is a connection between disobedience and lack of authority. One classic example is found in the book of Joshua. In Joshua 6, the great walled city is delivered into the hands of Israel as Israel obeyed the strange word of God to simply march around it. Shortly thereafter, in Joshua 7, Israel is defeated by the inferior military force at Ai because Achan, a member in Israel, did not obey the word of God.

This very clear connection between obedience and authority, and disobedience and the lack of authority, leads me to believe that the relative lack of authority in the healing ministry of the Western church is not only due to an inadequate theology and inappropriate models, but also due to the moral corruption, unbelief and disobedience in our corporate body. Leslie Weatherhead suggests that

> it may well be that the whole fellowship of the church needs to be raised to a higher spiritual level today before individual healers in it can repeat the healing activities of the Son of God, and that until groups within the church today are willing to pass through the same kind of discipline, the healing ministry of the church will be restricted.[2]

Jesus' Obedience and Authority

Obedience and authority are seen most clearly in Jesus. Through the perfect obedience of the Son of God, the King established his kingdom rule on earth. As a man fully under God's authority, Jesus, the last Adam, re-established the reign and rule of God which had been lost by the first Adam, "For just as through the disobedience of the one man the many were made sinners, so also through the obedience of the one man the many will be made righteous" (Rom 5:19).

The primary healing needed on earth (the healing of humanity's relationship to God) was achieved because one man obeyed. All the blessings we now receive from God (including physical healing) flows from the obedience of Jesus. The atoning life and death of Christ procured our forgiveness. Jesus "learned obedience from what he suffered" (Heb 5:8), and to his obedience we owe everything.

The hallmark of Jesus' earthly ministry was obedience. "My food," he said, "is to do the will of him who sent me and to finish his work" (Jn 4:34).

Because Jesus was a man under authority, he was authorized by God to exercise authority. And as he did, the world which had been cursed and demonized through Adam's disobedience began to be healed and restored. The elements (the wind and waves) became obedient to the command of Jesus. An abundance of food was provided for the multitudes, not by the sweat of man's face, but by the command of God's obedient agent.

Sickness, yet another symptom of Adam's original disobedience, was healed. Those who had been demonized were set free. Others who had died were given back their lives. The symptoms of disobedience were being healed because one man obeyed. A man was once again exercising God's authority over God's creation as was originally intended.

Something of this reality was perceived by the crowds which followed Jesus. Those who listened to Jesus speak and watched him work were continually amazed at his exercise of authority. The implication of Jesus' divine authority was not lost on Satan and his forces either.

Jesus went into the synagogue and began to teach. The people were amazed at his teaching, because he taught them as one who had authority, not as the teachers of the law. Just then a man in their synagogue who was possessed by an evil spirit cried out, "What do you want with us, Jesus of Nazareth? Have you come to destroy us? I know who you are—the Holy One of God!" (Mk 1:21-24)

Jesus' answer to the demon's question was, yes, he had come to destroy them. His mission was to undo the destructive rule of Satan, manifest in ignorance, alienation, hunger, sickness and bondage. And because Jesus was a man under God's authority, strictly following his orders, God backed up his words and deeds with power, making that authority effective.

The distinction between authority and power is subtle but significant in light of our present discussion. God has endowed every creature with a kind of power appropriate to each in varying degrees. Power is inherent in being and may be used by the creature as it chooses in a more or less autonomous manner. Authority, however, is not the possession of any creature. Strictly speaking, authority is not possessed at all; rather, it is exercised. In order to exercise authority, one must be related to God, in whom all authority resides and from whom it flows. That is to say, power may be expressed at will, but in order to exercise authority as Jesus did, one must be under the authority of the Father.

This reality was understood by the Roman centurion who had asked Jesus to heal his servant (Lk 7:1-10). The centurion was under the authority of Caesar, who backed up his authority. That is why he could say, "I myself am a man under authority, with soldiers under me. I tell this one, 'Go,' and he goes; I tell that one, 'Come,' and he comes" (Lk 7:8).

The centurion understood that his soldiers obeyed him, not because he was more powerful than his army, but because Rome itself stood behind his authority. He understood that Jesus was under an even higher authority. Therefore, he told Jesus, "Say the word, and my servant will be healed" (v. 7). The forces which caused sickness obeyed Jesus, not because in his humanness he possessed more power than they, but because God stood with him.

Jesus confessed that he could do nothing on his own or by himself (Jn 5:19-20). Jesus defeated Satan and destroyed his works of sickness and bondage, not because of a superior power inherent in him during his earthly ministry, but because he was obedient to God's authority and therefore could exercise it. This dynamic is apparent in the temptation of Christ (Mt 4). Jesus defeated Satan, not by an exercise of raw power, but by remaining under God's authority, submitting to his Word. Through obedience, Jesus exercised authority and by his authority defeated the works of the devil.

The Authority of Jesus' Followers

From the beginning, God intended for humanity to have dominion over the world (Gen 1:28). The lines of authority which were broken by Adam's disobedience have now been re-established by the second Adam, the Lord Jesus Christ. As he proclaims in Matthew 28:18, "All authority in heaven and on earth has been given to me." And this authority he gives to his church: "Go and make disciples of all nations, . . . teaching them to obey everything I have commanded you" (vv. 19-20). The lines of true authority were not only re-established by Christ but also extended by him into all the world through the church. The rule of God, that is to say the kingdom of God, was established by Jesus and is now expanded as we obey him.

In commenting on the connection between the church and the kingdom of God, Geerhardus Vos explains:

> Here again we must first of all insist upon it, that our Lord looked upon the visible Church as a veritable embodiment of His Kingdom. . . . We must say, therefore, that the Kingdom-forces which are at work, the Kingdom-life sphere, find expression in the Kingdom-organism of the visible Church.[3]

This truth is foreshadowed in Luke 9:1: "When Jesus had called the Twelve together, he gave them power and authority to drive out demons and to cure diseases." Likewise, to the rest of his followers

Jesus said, "I have given you authority to trample on snakes and scorpions and to overcome all the power of the enemy" (Lk 10:19).

When Jesus said that the gates of hell will not prevail against the church, he pictured Satan as a trapped and besieged enemy who is fighting a losing, defensive battle on all fronts. The boundaries of his pseudokingdom will constantly shrink as the church presses in. We are called to fight in a war we cannot lose. The church, however, does not win by default; it wins through active obedience. Despite the fact that Satan's pseudokingdom now stands in ruins, its influence remains unchecked if the church does not challenge it.

When we obey Christ, as he obeyed his Father, the authority he exercised will be evidenced in our ministries as well. Jesus explained in John 15 how this would work. "If you remain in me and my words remain in you, ask whatever you wish, and it will be given you" (v. 7). That is to say, "If you obey my commands, you will remain in my love, just as I have obeyed my Father's commands and remain in his love" (v. 10).

Jesus promises us authority over sickness and demonic forces. He assures us that the power that backs up that authority will be provided. But in John 15 we see that these promises and assurances are conditional. Only if we obey will we exercise authority.

That is not to suggest that obedience is some type of magic by which we force God to act, for that would be "faith formula" under another name. First, there will always be mystery in what God does and why. He does not answer to us for his actions nor does he always explain them. Second, until Christ's return all our ministry is partial, for now we only have a foretaste of what we will have perfectly then. And third, our obedience is never perfect. Great men and women of God confess that the closer they get to God and the more they obey him, the more they become aware of deeper levels of disobedience within themselves, levels they never dreamed existed. But none of this distracts from the fact that disobedience blocks authority to heal and simple trusting obedience is what God uses.

In the past few years, I have met many individuals like Tammy, who were not necessarily learned or wise, but who nevertheless exercised great authority in healing God's creatures. These people are vastly different from each other in age, education and circumstance, but they hold in common a desire to proclaim the good news of God's grace in Christ and a willingness to minister to the sick as he directs. I have often observed them risking comfort, reputation and even livelihood in their eagerness to exercise the authority Christ gave them.

As I was completing this book, a friend of mine phoned to report that in the course of his work as an appliance repairman, he called on a woman who was seriously sick in bed. Despite his embarrassment and the apparent inappropriateness of the occasion, he offered to pray for her. She cautiously accepted his offer. After he prayed for her, she got out of bed, surprised and relieved to be feeling better. By the time he finished repairing her dishwasher, she had completely recovered. He then told her about her need of salvation through Jesus Christ, who, as he explained, had just healed her. Needless to say, she was interested.

Another friend of mine who is a medical doctor risks his professional reputation by praying over some conditions for which drugs might normally be prescribed. This form of therapy often proves to be effective, but it is difficult to justify to his medical colleagues.

A pastor I know has jeopardized the excellent standing he has enjoyed within his denomination by introducing healing meetings into the life of his church. The meetings themselves did not cause as much tension among his peers as the fact that in those meetings people were actually healed and delivered of evil spirits.

I met a woman recently who works in a large downtown office building. She devotes her lunch breaks to praying for sick people. Her ministry is now in such demand that those who want her help must book appointments with her days in advance.

These individuals and hundreds of others I might have mentioned have discovered that, by following Christ in his ministry of proclamation and healing, they have been entrusted with the authority and power which make that ministry effective.

Christ does not will that the oppression and sickness all about us continue. Nor is he impotent before it. He is willing and he is powerful through the Holy Spirit to heal and to deliver. What he awaits is the obedience of his people. As John White and I concluded in our book *Healing the Wounded*:

Christ was indeed manifested. He did destroy the works of the devil. We need put up with Satan's schemes no longer. As followers of Christ we have authority to unleash his conquering sword, joining him in the completion of his devil-destroying conquest. . . .

It would be better to fight and lose than to allow the present situation to continue.

But there is no reason why we should lose. We are invited to run, sword in hand, in the steps of a conqueror.[4]

Notes

Introduction: Rediscovering the Ministry of Healing

[1] The Lausanne Occasional Paper No. 21, drafted under the chairmanship of the Rev. John R. W. Stott, identifies the signs of the kingdom of God as being crucial and essential to the evangelical gospel. The committee members state: "Evangelism is the proclamation of the kingdom in the fullness of its blessings and promise. . . . Jesus did more than preach the kingdom; he demonstrated its reality with 'signs of the kingdom,' public evidence that the kingdom he was talking about had come. We believe that signs should validate our evangelism, too"—*Evangelism and Social Responsibility,* Lausanne Occasional Paper No. 21 (Grand Rapids: 1982), pp. 31-32.

[2] J. Sidlow Baxter, *Divine Healing of the Body* (Grand Rapids: Zondervan, 1979); Morton Kelsey, *Healing and Christianity* (New York: Harper & Row, 1973).

Chapter 1: Sanctification through Sickness

[1] Francis MacNutt, *The Power to Heal* (Notre Dame: Ave Maria Press,

1977), pp. 139-40.

[2]Peter Davids, "Suffering in Biblical and Historical Perspective," unpublished manuscript, 1985.

[3]Morton Kelsey, *Healing and Christianity* (New York: Harper & Row, 1973), p. 16.

[4]Friedrich Nietzsche, *Twilight of the Idols and the Anti-Christ,* trans. R. J. Hallingdale (New York: Penguin Books, 1986), p. 167.

[5]J. I. Packer, Comments recorded in *Touchstone,* No. 2 (Richmond, B.C.: Riverbed Publishing, 1986), p. 7.

[6]Someone will wish to bring Job into our discussion at this point. True, Job is a stark reminder that there is mystery in human suffering and this should keep us humble about our orthodoxy on this point. However, we must also say that Job cannot be used in support of "sanctification through sickness." The principal reason is that God himself declared Job to be already "perfect" (KJV), that is to say he was "blameless and upright" (Job 1:8) prior to his affliction.

[7]In Hebrews 5:8, we read that although Jesus "was a son, he learned obedience from what he suffered." In Matthew 16:21, we hear Jesus "explain to his disciples that he must go to Jerusalem and suffer many things." Jesus anticipated suffering as a part of his mission, but what he expected was persecution, not sickness. We are told that as followers of Jesus, we may expect the same. "We are . . . heirs of God and co-heirs with Christ, if indeed we share in his sufferings" (Rom 8:17). "For just as the sufferings of Christ flow over into our lives, so also through Christ, our comfort overflows" (2 Cor 1:5). The potential value of suffering is very real to me. At age 21, I became a follower of Jesus, initially through painful and life-threatening circumstances. At age 25, I was locked up in an East European Communist prison for preaching the gospel and distributing Bibles. During that time of suffering I experienced a closeness to God that I would not trade for anything. Much of what I value in life came through suffering.

[8]Klaus Seybold, Ulrich B. Mueller, *Sickness and Healing,* trans. Douglas Stott (Nashville: Abingdon, 1981), p. 191.

[9]Paul speaks at length throughout his epistles of the true value of the suffering which includes persecution. This kind of spiritual, religious and political opposition is bound up in his teaching on dying with Christ. A helpful discussion of this is found in Rupert C. Tannehill's *Dying and Rising with Christ* (Berlin: Verlag Alfred Topelmann, n.d.), pp. 14-23.

Chapter 2: Divine Determinism

[1]Sidney Ahlstrom, *A Religious History of the American People*, Vol. 1 (New York: Image, 1975), p. 346.

[2]Russell Dicks, *Towards Health and Wholeness* (New York: MacMillan Co., 1960), p. 33.

[3]Leslie D. Weatherhead, *Psychology, Religion and Healing* (New York: Abingdon Press, 1951), p. 25.

Chapter 3: Faith Formula

[1]Charles Farah, "The Roots and Fruits of Faith Formula Theology," unpublished manuscript, 1980, p. 4.

[2]Thomas Smail, *The Forgotten Father* (Grand Rapids: Eerdmans, 1980), p. 154.

[3]Charles Farah, *From the Pinnacle of the Temple* (Plainfield, N.J.: Logos), p. 133.

[4]An example of current sermon titles from "faith formula" teachers.

[5]Gordon D. Fee, *The Disease of Health and Wealth Gospels* (Costa Mesa, Calif.: The Word for Today, 1979), p. 17.

[6]Smail, *Forgotten Father*, p. 142.

Chapter 4: The Secular World View

[1]Don Cupitt, *The World to Come* (London: SCM, 1982), pp. 54-55.

[2]David Hume, cited in Anthony Flew, *Western Philosophy* (New York: Bobbs-Merrill, 1971), p. 257.

[3]For a helpful discussion of various world views, I recommend James W. Sire, *The Universe Next Door* (Downers Grove, Ill.: InterVarsity Press, 1979).

[4]See material on Descartes in John Herman Randle, *The Making of the Modern Mind* (Cambridge, Mass.: Houghton Mifflin, 1940).

[5]Malachi Martin, *The Jesuits* (New York: The Linden Press, 1987), p. 259.

[6]Thomas McKlown, *Medical History and Medical Care* (London: Oxford Press, 1971), p. 36.

[7]C. S. Lewis, *God in the Dock* (Grand Rapids: Eerdmans, 1970), p. 25.

[8]Weatherhead, *Psychology, Religion and Healing*, p. 459.

[9]Ibid., p. 32.

Part II: The Kingdom of God and the Fight to Heal

[1]Michael Green, *I Believe in Satan's Downfall* (London: Hodder and

Stoughton, 1981), p. 208.

[2]James Kallas, *The Significance of the Synoptic Gospels* (Greenwich, Conn.: Seabury Press, 1961), p. 86.

Chapter 5: God Desires to Heal the Sick

[1]J. I. Packer, *Knowing God* (Downers Grove, Ill.: InterVarsity Press, 1973), p. 113.

[2]Thomas F. Torrance, *The Mediation of Christ* (Grand Rapids: Eerdmans, 1983), pp. 32-33.

[3]Leon Morris, *The Gospel according to John* (Grand Rapids: Eerdmans, 1971), p. 114.

[4]Stephen Neill, *Jesus through Many Eyes* (Philadelphia: Fortress Press, 1976), p. 145.

[5]Karl Barth, *Church Dogmatics*, IV/2, trans. G. W. Bromiley (Edinburgh: T. & T. Clark, 1967), p. 223.

[6]Hugh Martin, *Luke's Portrait of Jesus* (London: SCM Press, 1949), p. 64.

[7]Charles Hartshorne, *Omnipotence and Other Theological Mistakes* (New York: State University Press, 1984), p. 27.

[8]Abraham Heschel, *The Prophets*, Vol. 2 (New York: Harper & Row, 1962), p. 88.

Chapter 6: The Assault of the Kingdom of God

[1]George Eldon Ladd, *The Gospel of the Kingdom* (Grand Rapids: Eerdmans, 1959), p. 47.

[2]Kenneth Leech, *Soul Friend* (San Francisco: Harper & Row, 1977), p. 132.

[3]Herman Ridderbos, *The Coming of the Kingdom*, trans. H. de Jongste, (Grand Rapids: Baker, 1962), p. 67.

[4]Werner Foerster, "[daimon]," in *Theological Dictionary of the New Testament*, 10 vols., ed. Gerhard Kittel and Gerhard Friedrich, trans. G. W. Bromiley (Grand Rapids: Eerdmans, 1964-76), 2:18.

[5]Leech, *Soul Friend*, p. 132.

[6]Peter R. Kowey, M.D., Ted D. Friehling, M.D., and Roger A. Marinchak, M.D., "Prayer-Meeting Cardioversion": (Philadelphia: The Medical College of Pennsylvania, n.d.) Letter 727.

[7]E. M. B. Green, *The Meaning of Salvation* (London: Hodder and Stoughton, 1965), p. 112.

[8]Raymond Brown, *New Testament Essays* (London: Chapman, 1965), p. 174.

Chapter 7: The Fight Is Real

[1]Thomas A. Smail, *Reflected Glory* (Grand Rapids: Eerdmans, 1975), p. 124.

[2]Dorothy L. Sayers, *The Devil to Pay* (London: Victor Gollanez, 1939), p. 100.

[3]Sir John Eccles and Daniel N. Robinson, *The Wonder of Being Human* (Boston: Shambhala, 1985), pp. 99-100.

[4]Colin Brown, *Miracles and the Critical Mind* (Grand Rapids: Eerdmans, 1984), p. 15.

[5]G. C. Berkouwer, *Sin,* trans. Phillip Holtrop, Studies in Dogmatics (Grand Rapids: Eerdmans, 1971), pp. 121-22.

Chapter 8: Our Faith in the Fight

[1]Gayle D. Erwin, *The Jesus Style* (Palm Springs: Ronald N. Haynes Publisher, 1983), p. 136.

[2]John Bright, *The Kingdom of God* (Nashville: Abingdon, 1953), pp. 127-185; George Eldon Ladd, *The Presence of the Future* (Grand Rapids: Eerdmans, 1974), pp. 76-101.

[3]Ladd, *Presence of the Future,* p. 77.

[4]Ibid., p. 95.

[5]Ladd, *Gospel of the Kingdom,* pp. 56-57.

[6]Smail, *Reflected Glory,* p. 101.

Chapter 9: The Victory Present and Future

[1]Bright, *Kingdom of God* (Nashville: Abingdon, 1953), p. 218.

[2]Ladd, *Presence of the Future,* p. 217.

[3]Ray Anderson, *On Being Human* (Grand Rapids: Eerdmans, 1982), pp. 204-5.

[4]Ladd, *Gospel of the Kingdom,* p. 139.

Chapter 10: Models of Healing

[1]C. Peter Wagner, "Healing without Hassle," *Leadership,* 7, No. 2 (Spring 1985):114.

[2]It is beyond the scope of this book to review the approaches to healing found in each of these traditions and at the same time do them justice. Anyone wishing to learn what God has taught the church about healing over the years and how his Spirit is healing through the church today need only visit a well-stocked Christian book store. Conspicuously absent from the shelves will be much on healing from a mainstream evangelical

perspective.

Chapter 11: Getting Started

[1]Wimber's own discussion of this model can be found in John Wimber and Kevin Springer, *Power Healing* (San Francisco: Harper & Row, 1986).

[2]Paul Tournier, *The Healing of Persons,* trans. Edwin Hudson (New York: Harper & Row, 1965).

[3]Cited by Karen Granberg-Michaelson, *The Land of the Living* (Grand Rapids: Zondervan, 1984), p. 41.

[4]O. Carl Simonton, Stephanie Mathews-Simonton and James L. Creighton, *Getting Well Again* (New York: Bantam, 1978).

[5]Frederick Buechner, *Wishful Thinking* (New York: Harper & Row, 1973), p. 37

[6]For a theological and practical treatment of this subject, see John White and Ken Blue, *Healing the Wounded: The Costly Love of Church Discipline* (Downers Grove, Ill.: InterVarsity Press, 1985).

Chapter 12: Wholeness and Healing in Three Dimensions

[1]The fact that our present bodies die to make way for ones which will not die should keep us from joining with some health and fitness zealots who make physical health an absolute and ultimate value. In praying for the sick we remember that on the one hand every healing is partial and provisional—each body healed now will die later. On the other hand no failure to be healed is an ultimate disaster for the Christian because the work of Christ which is not manifest on this side of the grave will be realized on the other side.

[2]See Peter Davids, "A Working Model for Healing: The Holistic Approach" (Regent College, 2130 Westbrook Mall, Vancouver, B.C., Canada).

Chapter 13: Obedience and the Authority to Heal

[1]Francis MacNutt, *Healing* (Notre Dame, Ind.: Ave Maria Press, 1974), p. 134.

[2]Weatherhead, *Psychology, Religion and Healing,* p. 32.

[3]Geerhardus Vos, *The Teaching of Jesus concerning the Kingdom of God and the Church* (Phillipsburg, N. J.: Presbyterian and Reformed Publishing Co., 1972), pp. 86-87.

[4]White and Blue, *Healing the Wounded,* p. 209.

How To Have A Healing Ministry Without Making Your Church Sick

by C Peter Wagner

Should traditional evangelical churches remain apart from the charismatic renewal?

Peter Wagner believes that there have been three distinct 'waves' of God's Spirit in the twentieth century. The first was the Pentecostal movement, the second the charismatic movement. The third wave is now under way, as the Spirit manifests the same kind of power in traditional evangelical churches, but without requiring them to abandon their distinctive nature—to 'make themselves sick'.

As Dr Wagner analyses how the conservative evangelical churches are finding a new vitality of faith, he describes how, from being vehemently anti-charismatic, he has come to recognise the value of charismatic ministry and ultimately to exercise a significant healing gift himself, though without joining a charismatic church.

Dr Peter Wagner is Professor of Church Growth at Fuller Theological Seminary. He has written many books, including Your Spiritual Gifts Can Help Your Church Grow and Leading Your Church To Growth.

Monarch
Publications